DISEASES

2nd Revised Edition

Volume 2

Blood to Crohn's disease

Bryan Bunch

EDITOR
SCIENTIFIC PUBLISHING

GROLIER
EDUCATIONAL

Editor: Bryan Bunch

Design and production: G & H SOHO, Inc.
Design: Gerry Burstein
Prepress: Kathie Kounouklos

Writers:

Barbara Branca
Bryan Bunch
Barbara A. Darga
Betsy Feist
Gene R. Hawes
Wendy B. Murphy
Karin L. Rhines
Jenny Tesar
Bruce Wetterau
Gray Williams

Editorial assistant:
Marianne Bunch

Copyediting and index:
Felice Levy

Creative assistance:
Pam Forde

Illustrators:

Photographs:
Karin L. Rhines

Icons:
Steve Virkus and Karen Presser

Medical Illustrations:
Jean Cassels
Leslie Dunlap
Pamela Johnson
Joel Snyder

Library of Congress Cataloging in Publication Data

Main entry under title:
Diseases
v. < >' cm
Includes bibliographical references and index.
Summary: Alphabetically arranged articles present medical information
on more than 500 diseases, discussing causes, symptoms, stages of the
disease, its likelihood of striking, treatments, prevention, and long-term effects.

Set ISBN: 0-7172-5688-X
1. Diseases—Encyclopedias, Juvenile. [1. Diseases—
Encyclopedias.] I. Grolier Educational Corporation
R130.5 D57 1996
616.003—dc20   96-27606
                                        CIP
                                        AC

Revised edition published 2003.
First published in the United States in 1997 by
Grolier Educational, Sherman Turnpike, Danbury, CT 06816

COPYRIGHT © 2003, 1997 by SCIENTIFIC PUBLISHING, INC.

A HUDSON GROUP BOOK

Set ISBN: 0-7172-5688-X

Volume ISBN: 0-7172-5690-1

Blood

Blood is a complex substance that contains several different kinds of cells suspended in a fluid that is filled with various proteins and other chemicals. The mix of water and chemicals that remains when cells are removed is a clear yellow liquid called *plasma* (PLAAZ-muh) or (when separated from proteins involved in clotting) *serum* (SIHR-uhm).

Location and amount: Blood is the body's only liquid organ. It is normally inside veins and arteries throughout the body, which together form the *bloodstream*. The smallest passages for blood, the capillaries, have such thin walls that parts of blood pass through them when needed; for example, disease-fighting cells can leave the bloodstream. But if a break in the bloodstream occurs, such as a cut or even a small tear in an artery, escaped whole blood can be dangerous to the cells nearby, largely because of the pressure it can exert on them.

The normal amount of blood in a human is about 10 to 12 pounds in a person weighing around 150 pounds. A man has more blood than a woman of the same weight. A 150-pound man has about 11 or 12 pints of blood, while a woman of that weight has only 8 or 9 pints, and a woman weighing less has even less, with 7 pints about the average.

Blood is constantly on the move. In 20 seconds a specific drop of blood can circulate completely from the heart, through the body, and back to the heart. That is because blood travels at an average rate of 0.7 miles per hour.

Role: Different parts of blood have different functions. The red color of blood comes from *erythrocytes* (ih-RIHTH-ruh-SIYTZ), commonly known as *red blood cells*. Erythrocytes lack nuclei and internal structure. They are produced by cells in the bone marrow (called *stem cells*) for just one purpose—to carry needed oxygen to cells and to remove carbon dioxide, which is produced when cells use the oxygen.

Marrow stem cells also make several varieties of *white blood cells,* such as lymphocytes and phagocytes, which are important parts of the immune system that fights invading bacteria, virusus, or funguses.

Another component of blood made by marrow stem cells

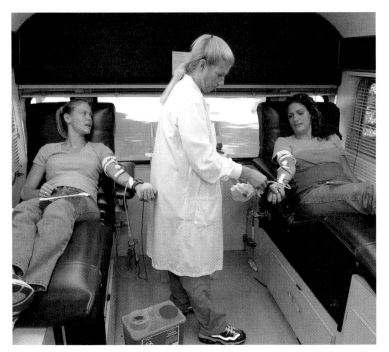

Healthy persons are able to stay healthy with a somewhat smaller amount of blood than is normally in their circulatory system, and the body quickly replaces any lost. Many illnesses can be alleviated with whole blood or with parts of blood, such as plasma or antibodies, and accident victims often lose much of their blood supply, so donated blood has been a major factor in saving lives in the past century. Here students from Purdue University in Indiana donate blood in response to the 9/11 terrorist attacks on the United States in 2001. (Purdue News Service Photo by David Umberger)

is the *platelets*. Their function is to keep blood from flowing out of the body by producing clotting if there is a break in the walls of the circulatory system.

Proteins in the blood serum include several involved in producing blood clots, produced by the platelets, and antibodies, produced by white blood cells, which help defend against specific diseases.

Conditions that affect the blood: Most blood diseases attack blood cells, but many in other parts of the body can also alter blood chemistry. When blood becomes too acid or alkaline, or when it contains an insufficient amount of certain important minerals, especially sodium and potassium, the body can no longer depend on blood as a ready supply of necessary materials for cell functioning. If not corrected, such a chemical imbalance in the blood can lead to serious illness or even death. Often the cause of such an imbalance is sweating that is not compensated for by drinking enough liquids, although chemical imbalances can also be caused by diseases of the kidneys or liver, two organs that regularly adjust conditions in the blood.

Blood cells are manufactured from the stem cells of bone

marrow, so conditions that affect these stem cells result in defective blood. Such conditions include several forms of cancer, for which leukemia is the general name, since these cancers mostly affect the white blood cells (*leuke-* means "white"). Red blood cells are subject to genetic disorders and deficiency diseases, classed as anemias. In some diseases chemicals, bacteria, viruses, or parasites interfere with or destroy specific kinds of blood cells. The best-known diseases are AIDS (a virus infects certain white blood cells) and malaria (a parasite infects red blood cells). Some diseases also reduce the number of platelets.

A combination of the volume of blood, the activity of the heart, and the condition and activity of the arteries is necessary to maintain enough, but not too much, blood throughout the body. This combination is measured as *blood pressure*. Blood pressure rises and falls with each heartbeat, so it is measured as two numbers, such as 120 over 80. Blood pressure that is too high damages some organs, including the kidneys and the heart, while low blood pressure can cause *fainting* or, if very low, *shock*. High blood pressure can also contribute to damage to arteries that leads to aneurysm, bleeding, or stroke.

Blood poisoning

DISEASE

TYPE: INFECTIOUS
(BACTERIAL)

Phone doctor

The medical name for blood poisoning is *septicemia* (SEHP-tih-SEE-mee-uh) or *sepsis,* or in mild cases, *bacteremia* (BAAK-tuh-REE-mee-uh). Septicemia is not a form of poisoning at all but a bacterial infection that spreads through the circulatory system. In some cases, however, the infecting bacteria do produce a poison (called a *toxin*) as part of their attack on the body. Because the bacteria are being spread by the body's own method for internal transportation, they can reach any organ. As a result, blood poisoning can be very dangerous. ***If blood poisoning is suspected, seek medical attention immediately.***

Cause: Any break in the circulatory system, including a minor cut, can introduce bacteria into the blood. The most serious cases of blood poisoning begin when the break involves a localized sore, such as a boil, that breaks through to the blood. Although many different kinds of bacteria can spread through the blood, the common ones are *Streptococcus* and *Staphylococcus*.

Incidence: Since bacteria are found everywhere, unless a wounded area has been sterilized, they enter blood every time there is a cut. But in most cases the body's immune system quickly defeats invading bacteria. Despite this protection, septicemia is the twelfth leading cause of death in the United States. By far the people most at risk are those over 65 years of age. The rate for young persons (15 to 44 years old) is about 5% of that for senior citizens. Septicemia strikes newborns as well.

Noticeable symptoms: Blood poisoning produces symptoms of shock, including chills and a pale, clammy appearance. There is usually a high fever and sometimes visible eruptions on the skin.

Diagnosis: Blood pressure often falls rapidly in cases of blood poisoning. A physician who suspects septicemia will perform a quick test, called a white-blood-cell count, on a sample of blood. If there are many more white blood cells than usual, it means that the body is fighting an invasion. The blood sample may be cultured to determine the specific bacterium that is causing the disease.

Treatment options: Before antibiotics septicemia was a common cause of death. Today if septicemia is detected early enough, antibiotics usually clear it up completely. Sometimes, however, bacteria become resistant to commonly used antibiotics, and a second or even third medicine must be employed. Untreated septicemia can soon become too severe to stop and will become fatal.

Vaccination to prevent infection by *Haemophilus* (hee-MOF-ih-luhs) *B* bacteria, routine in the United States, lowers the risk. People with an immune system compromised by damage to the spleen should also be vaccinated against pneumonia.

Stages and progress: Blood poisoning can induce pockets of infection (abscesses) in any of the major organs that interfere with their functions, but septicemia by itself can kill by producing toxins that cause shock and kidney failure.

Prevention and risk factors: Cuts and abrasions should always be washed with soap and water to eliminate as many bacteria as possible. Surgical procedures, especially involving boils or abscesses, can also produce blood poisoning. Urinary tract infections often lead to blood poisoning, either on their own or when a catheter is introduced.

Boils

DISEASE

TYPE: INFECTIOUS
(BACTERIAL)

See also
**AIDS
(acquired immunodeficiency
syndrome)**
Bacteria and disease
Blood poisoning
**Diabetes mellitus, type I
("juvenile")**
**Diabetes mellitus, type II
("adult onset")**
Phagocytes
"Staph"

Phone doctor

A boil is an inflamed, pus-filled swelling of the skin. A cluster of boils connected beneath the skin is called a *carbuncle* (KAAR-buhng-kuhl). Physicians sometimes call boils *furuncles* (FYOO-ruhng-kuhls).

Cause: Boils are caused by certain bacteria, especially *Staphylococcus*. The bacteria usually infect a hair follicle (the "root"). White blood cells, which are part of the body's defense system, move into the area to fight the bacteria. This produces white or yellow pus, which consists of white blood cells, bacteria, and dead skin cells.

Incidence: Boils are very common, appearing most often on the face, neck, breasts, and buttocks. Some people who are otherwise healthy develop recurrent boils. Carbuncles also occur in otherwise healthy people. Males frequently develop carbuncles on the back of the neck. People with lowered resistance to infection, including those with diabetes mellitus or AIDS, have an increased susceptibility to carbuncles.

Noticeable symptoms: A boil begins as a red, tender lump. Over the period of one to two days it fills with pus, becoming larger and more painful. Usually it continues to grow for a week or longer, until it bursts.

Sometimes bacteria from a boil enter the blood and are carried to other parts of the body. The spreading infection, or blood poisoning, may cause fever, chills, and swollen lymph nodes. ***If this occurs, it is important to see a doctor as soon as possible.*** It also is important to see a doctor if a boil is large or persists for several weeks or more, and if you have recurrent boils, a condition called *furunculosis* (FYOO-ruhng-kuh-LOH-sihs).

Treatment options: Apply hot, damp cloths to the boil to relieve pain and to hasten bursting and drainage. If a boil is large and painful, a doctor may open it with a sterile needle or knife to drain the pus. If you have recurrent boils, the doctor may prescribe antibiotics and the use of an antiseptic soap.

Bone diseases

Bone is one of the great inventions of evolution. Most animals are tiny invertebrates, unable to become large because they either have no hard parts or grow inside nonliving shells of one kind or another. The largest invertebrate, the giant squid, can grow outside a small inner shell because its body is buoyed by immersion in water. But vertebrates—including fish, amphibians, reptiles, birds, and mammals—are built around a living framework of bone that grows with them, supporting and protecting the organs of the body.

Although bones contain much material that is more mineral than animal, they also include living cells in their marrow. Other living cells create the bone that surrounds them. Even the mineral part of bone can be added to or subtracted from by bone cells as the needs of the body change. As a result, any disease or disorder that causes some bones to grow too fast or to lose too much mineral matter results in damage. Furthermore, some diseases of cells in bone adversely affect other parts of the body.

Framework of the body: Just as a modern skyscraper is hung on a framework of steel girders, the body of a human or other vertebrate is supported by a framework of bone. When a disease causes bone to lose or change its mineral content, the damaged framework leads to collapse of part of the body. Bone that is brittle or soft can break easily, for example. When bones in the spine collapse, the spinal cord becomes partly crushed, causing intense pain. In some cases a person visibly shrinks as loss of support causes the body to collapse a little at a time.

The initial processes of development by which bone is formed before birth may be defective for any number of reasons. This may result in bones that are poorly shaped or even absent. Such birth defects range in severity from disfiguring but not life-threatening deformities, such as cleft palate or clubfoot, to conditions that almost invariably lead to death at a very young age.

Protected inner part: The most vital organs in the body are protected by hard bone. The brain inside the skull and the heart and lungs within the rib cage are the most obvious examples. But deep inside the long bones themselves, in one of the most protected parts of the body, lie the stem cells of the marrow. These bone cells produce the key elements of one of the least protected vital organs, red and white blood cells and platelets. If a person loses a lot of blood but escapes death, the stem cells can replenish the loss in a short time. But if a person loses the stem cells, blood gradually loses its functions of carrying oxygen, fighting disease, and clotting to close wounds. Such a loss is invariably fatal unless the stem cells are replaced.

Bacterial diseases: Bacteria grow almost everywhere, including on bone. The worst damage comes from certain bacteria from diseases that also infect different parts of the body. Such bacteria are often harder to eradicate from bone than from other organs. Tuberculosis is among the bacterial diseases that can infect bone, causing particular damage when the characteristic sores appear on the bones of the spine (*Pott's disease)*. Several spirochete bacteria, which cause such diseases as syphilis, Lyme disease, and yaws, are also capable of infecting bone.

Paget's disease: Viruses grow and reproduce only inside living cells, so most viruses do not have the devastating effect on the hard parts of bone that some bacteria do. *Paget's* (PAAJ-ihts) *disease*, however, which may affect as many as 3% of those over 55 in the United States, may be caused by a virus—although no specific culprit has been found. The virus seemingly infects cells that normally release minerals from bone. The infection causes destruction of hard parts of bone, but overcompensation by other types of cells causes bones to thicken. Such thickening may lead to arthritis or even to brain damage if the skull is affected.

For unknown reasons men are more often affected by Paget's disease than women, Europeans more than Americans, and people in North America and Europe more than people living in Asia, Africa, or South America.

Cancer: Most bone cancers originate somewhere else in the body and then spread to bones, where they are very difficult to stop. The bone cancer that is a common complication of prostate cancer is more likely to cause death than the original prostate tumor, for example.

Mechanical disorders: Mechanical disorders are caused when physical—not biological or chemical—problems produce a disorder. Bones, both the body's rigid support and system of hinges and bearings, are especially likely candidates for mechanical disorders.

Even healthy bones can break, but they will heal themselves. A physician often must direct the healing process with a splint or cast to ensure that the new bone will grow straight and strong.

Overuse of the body can cause other forms of wear and tear, including *Osgood-Schlatter* (OZ-guud SHLAA-tuhr) *disease,* a partial separation of parts of the knee in young athletes, and osteoarthritis, joint wear in older persons. Mechanical bone problems can often be treated with surgery, including replacement of joints. Obese people may reduce symptoms of osteoarthritis by losing weight.

Some of the "osteo-" disorders

The Greek word for a bone was *osteon,* so the combining form *osteo-* is frequently used in medicine for conditions that affect the bones. It can sometimes be difficult to remember which condition is which, although some are relatively easy to figure out.

- *Osteoarthritis* sounds as if it is "arthritis of the bones." It is a painful condition caused by the wearing away of bone and cartilage at joints. Since it is caused by mechanical wear and tear, it mainly affects older people.
- *Osteoporosis* is also common among older people, especially older women. The word ending *-porosis* is the same base word as *porous.* The name indicates that the bones are becoming porous, or filled with holes, like a sponge. The bones also become brittle and weak. It is thought that the main problem is a lack of calcium in the bones.
- *Osteomalacia* is a condition similar to osteoporosis, but caused by lack of vitamin D. The Greek word *malakia* means softness. Vitamin D is needed to incorporate calcium into bone, so both osteomalacia and osteoporosis are conditions in which there is too little calcium. Sometimes *osteomalacia* is used to mean bone that has lost a different mineral, phosphorous.
- *Osteomyelitis* gets its name by combining the Greek *osteon* with *myel,* a Latin form based on the Greek word for bone marrow, and the familiar medical suffix *-itis,* meaning "inflammation." In osteomyelitis, just as its name indicates, inflammation of the bone marrow is the main problem.
- *Osteosarcoma* (os-tee-oh-sahr-KOH-muh) is a cancer that originates in bone—a sarcoma is a cancer that originates in muscles or connective tissue. Osteosarcoma tends to strike young persons more than older ones—*Ewing's sarcoma* most often attacks the bones of people between the ages of 10 and 20.
- The name *osteogenesis imperfecta* suggests that bone is not completely formed. That is a good inference, since this condition is largely poor formation of cartilage and bone.

Bones

Bones are harder than most other parts of the body and contain much matter that is not alive. Despite their hardness, bones are often broken in accidents; they can also be affected by many different conditions and diseases. The combining form *osteo-*, which means "bone," is often used in the names of diseases that affect bone.

Size and location: There are normally 206 bones in the human body, forming the *skeleton*. Bones support all parts of the body and protect the brain and organs of the chest. Bones of the leg can be nearly 2 feet long, but the tiny bones of the middle ear are less than an eighth of an inch long, with the rest of the skeleton in between in size.

Role: The main function of the bones is to provide support and protection, but bones also have other vital functions. They are part of the circulatory system, for example, since inside bones a soft tissue called red marrow produces most of the body's blood cells. Bones are also part of the hormonal system. They are an important reservoir for minerals such as calcium. If the body's intake of calcium is too low, the bones release some of the calcium that is the main mineral in bone to make up the deficit. The loss of calcium weakens bones, however, making them more easily breakable.

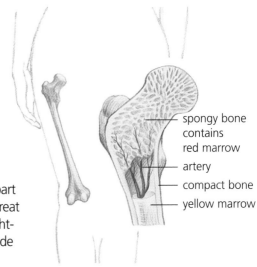

spongy bone contains red marrow
artery
compact bone
yellow marrow

Inside a bone
The spongy-looking inner part of limb bones gives bone great strength combined with lightness, while the marrow inside produces blood cells.

Conditions that affect bone: Diseases that affect bones are discussed in the article "Bone diseases." Bone cancer is a serious complication of many other cancers. Cancer is discussed further in the entry "Cancers."

A break in a bone is called a *fracture*. If part of the broken bone cuts through the skin, the break is a *compound fracture*. Broken bones grow back together if the broken parts stay close to each other, so physicians use various devices to hold bones in place while a break heals.

Botulism

(BOCH-uh-LIHZ-uhm)

DISEASE

TYPE: BACTERIAL
        POISONING

See also
Bacteria and disease
Food poisoning

Eating food contaminated by the botulism bacteria could be fatal. However, the bacteria themselves are not poisonous. Instead, they produce a highly toxic substance that causes the serious illness.

Cause: Eating improperly prepared canned foods is the most common cause of botulism. That is because the botulism bacterium, *Clostridium botulinum*, grows only in places with no free oxygen gas—such as a sealed can or jar of home preserves.

Spores of botulism bacteria are common in the soil and may cling to raw vegetables or other fresh foods. If the food containing these spores is canned without sufficient boiling, the spores become living botulism bacteria after the can or jar is sealed. As the bacteria multiply in that oxygen-free environment, they give off the powerful toxin that contaminates the food. If the food is eaten, the poison acts on the nervous system by blocking the electrical impulses that make muscles contract. The toxin also causes salivary glands to cease functioning.

Two other types of botulism have been discovered in recent years. *Wound botulism* occurs when botulism spores lodge deep in an unclean wound, multiply, and give off the toxin. *Infant botulism* strikes babies between two weeks and nine months old. Spores in honey or in processed baby foods lodge in the baby's intestine, where they can become living bacteria and give off their deadly toxin.

Incidence: Thanks to the general use of safe canning and preserving procedures, botulism poisoning is rare, with only about 350 cases a year reported in the United States. Outbreaks occur only sporadically, although some foods in certain countries are more susceptible to contamination. Canned vegetables, especially mushrooms, beans, and peppers, are the most common causes of botulism outbreaks in the United States. In Germany, France, and Poland most outbreaks come from eating canned meats. In Russia and Japan pickled and home-preserved fish are the leading culprits. Drug abuse involving injection of black tar heroin has led to more cases of wound botulism in recent years.

Noticeable symptoms: The early symptoms are severe but may not appear until half a day or, rarely, as many as eight days after eating food contaminated with botulism. They include abdominal pain, vomiting, headache, blurred or double vision, slurred speech, a feeling of weakness, retention of urine, constipation, and difficulty in breathing, swallowing, and even speaking. (All are caused by muscle failure.) ***Botulism can be fatal if medical treatment is delayed. Get immediate medical attention.*** Without medical treatment paralysis of legs and arms can follow. Death usually results from respiratory failure in untreated cases.

Call ambulance

Infants experiencing botulism poisoning show characteristic "floppy baby" symptoms of general weakness and listlessness.

Diagnosis: Based on respiratory problems and other symptoms, a physician may suspect botulism poisoning. Examination can reveal paralyzed eye or throat muscles. A blood test can confirm this diagnosis by showing toxin in the blood, but sometimes it is necessary to perform additional tests to rule out other possible causes of paralysis.

Treatment options: Treatment should begin as soon as possible. An emergency medical service (EMS) should be called immediately. If you know cardiopulmonary resuscitation (CPR), it should be practiced to keep oxygen flowing into the lungs if breathing difficulties appear while waiting for EMS. Anyone who has eaten the suspected food, whether showing symptoms or not, should be given emergency care.

Use CPR

Doctors induce vomiting to clear out any contaminated food in the stomach and flush out the patient's intestinal tract. An antitoxin for botulism helps counter the effects of the poison. If muscle paralysis is severe, a respirator may be needed to help with breathing.

More than three out of four persons who develop botulism poisoning eventually recover completely with proper care.

Prevention: To safeguard against botulism poisoning, follow safe, sensible rules whenever preparing, storing, and preserving food. Food in cans that are swollen or dented should never be eaten. Many foods have special pop tops that show that they are safe; if the top pops up, the food is contaminated. *If you suspect any canned food could be bad, throw it away.* In a food store notify the manager of any cans that look dangerous.

Boiling breaks down botulism toxins. Always bring canned foods, especially soups and nonacidic foods (such as beans), to a full boil when heating them prior to serving them. Home-canned foods should be boiled for ten minutes before serving.

Never give infants unpasteurized honey. Always wash out wounds with soap and water; any that are deep should also be treated with a bactericide (a medicine that kills bacteria).

Bowel obstruction

DISEASE

TYPE: MECHANICAL

See also
Back and spine problems
Digestive system
Gallstones
Hernias
Ileitis
Kidney and bladder stones
Large intestine
Peritonitis
Pregnancy and disease
Small intestine
Tumor, benign

Bowel obstruction, also known as *ileus* (IHL-ee-uhs), is the stoppage of onward movement of the food-derived materials passing through the intestine. It results from any kind of blockage or from spasms or paralysis of a part of the intestine. Ileus occurs infrequently, but its onset often requires emergency treatment.

Cause: Bowel obstruction can result from any of three causes.

■ Any sort of mechanical blockage or obstruction, including *adhesion* following surgery—an adhesion is a joining together of two parts of the body by scar tissue. The intestine may become bent back or twisted, an obstruction termed a *volvulus* (VOL-vyuh-luhs). A stone from the gallbladder, or even something indigestible that was eaten, can enter and block the intestine.

■ Pressure on the intestine from an adjacent organ, most commonly a uterus distended by pregnancy. Other possible blockages of this type include a hernia through which the intestine protrudes or a tumor that presses on the intestine.

- Any breakdown in normal functioning of the intestine, such as muscular paralysis or spasm or nerve impairment that stops the intestinal action that moves material onward. Such nerve impairment may appear in connection with peritonitis, complications with kidney stones or gallstones, or injury to the spinal cord.

Noticeable symptoms: Sharp pain in the abdomen coming first in spasms but later as uninterrupted pain is one of the first signs of bowel obstruction. Other signs include constipation, vomiting (which may include feces), and swelling of the abdomen. Severe dehydration and shock can develop not long after the outbreak of symptoms unless the condition is relieved by prompt treatment.

Diagnosis: Applying a stethoscope to the abdomen will reveal to a doctor the absence of any bowel sounds in a person with ileus. Such bowel sounds are constantly present in normal health. Abdominal x-rays of someone with bowel obstruction usually exhibit curved portions of intestine badly swollen by ballooning gases.

Treatment: Prompt treatment of bowel obstruction to relieve intestinal pressure is important in order to prevent perforation of the intestinal wall. *A person with ileus should not eat or drink.* Essential body fluids normally provided by intestinal action may need to be supplied intravenously.

A usual first step in treatment is to pump out the contents of the stomach. Intestinal pressure may be relieved by applying suction through a tube to the obstruction. This procedure may be sufficient to restore intestinal functioning that has been interrupted by a cause such as paralysis. Surgery may eventually be necessary in order to clear an obstruction.

No food

Brain

BODY SYSTEM

Thought by some ancient Greeks to be merely an "air conditioner" for the blood, the brain is known today as the main part of the central nervous system, controlling all parts of the body. The brain also records and interprets information from the senses, stores that information in itself as memory, participates in emotions, and in humans at least, thinks. If a human were a computer, the brain would be all of the chips, from the memory chips to the central processing unit.

Size and location: Located in the head, the brain is protected by the bones of the skull. There are two parts to the brain, called *hemispheres.* Each hemisphere is about 6 inches long from the front of the head to the back. The distance across the pair from left to right is about 4½ inches. Below the hemispheres a single *brain stem,* about 3 inches long, connects the brain to the *spinal cord,* which is connected to most of the rest of the nervous system. The nerves of the head, however, are connected directly to the brain. The brain itself weighs about 3 pounds.

Role: The brain is composed of several parts. The *cerebrum* (SEHR-uh-bruhm) is the folded outer part of each hemisphere. Its outer layer, the *cerebral cortex* (SEHR-uh-bruhl KAWR-tehks), governs thought, the senses, and movement. The cerebral cortex is less than 0.25-inch thick but deeply folded, so that if it were spread out flat, it would be about a yard square.

The two hemispheres of the *cerebellum* (SEHR-uh-BEHL-uhm) control balance and muscle coordination. The two halves of the brain are connected by the *corpus callosum* (kuh-LOH-suhm). Deep in the brain the brain stem governs involuntary muscles. A small, but important, part of the brain is the *hypothalamus* (HIY-poh-THAAL-uh-muhs), which controls the hormonal system. Various other small regions in the brain that have specific functions have been identified.

Conditions that affect the brain: Almost any disease affects the brain to some degree, but for most diseases the effect is indirect: pain and fatigue caused by disease, for example, are felt in the brain, manifested as headache or mental weariness. A sort of fence, called the *blood-brain barrier,* keeps many agents of disease and their products from reaching the brain itself.

The heavy skull is designed to protect the brain from injury, but often a sharp blow can bruise the brain against the inside of the skull; or the skull may be broken, and part of the bone or swelling can press against the brain. Any pressure or damage to the brain interferes with its function. Memories may be lost, limbs may become paralyzed, or death may result from damage to different parts of the brain.

The two hemispheres of the brain have been mapped. Different parts of the cerebrum handle different responses to the environment. The corpus callosum connects the hemispheres. Deep in the brain the hypothalamus controls body temperature, appetite, and the nearby pituitary gland, which in turn uses its hormone production to influence growth, energy use, sexual development, and reproduction.

senses
movement
behavior and emotion
HEMISPHERES of CEREBRUM
hands
personality
thought
speech
hearing
smell
vision
memory
CEREBELLUM

skull
cerebrum
corpus callosum
hypothalamus
pituitary gland
cerebellum
brain stem
spinal cord

The nervous system, including the brain, uses chemical messengers to communicate with its different parts. Too much or too little of a particular messenger in the brain can cause serious disease, including some severe mental illnesses called *psychoses* (siy-KOH-seez).

Development of the brain can be affected in various ways. Some genetic disorders impair the formation of the brain to one degree or another, often during the fetal stages of growth, but sometimes well into adulthood. A few diseases, such as rubella or alcoholism, and some vitamin deficiencies in a mother can also interfere with fetal development of the brain. When the brain is affected before birth or in early years, mental ability may be impaired.

Brain abscess

DISEASE

TYPE: MECHANICAL

See also
Abscess
Bacteria and disease
Brain
Dental illnesses and conditions

Call ambulance

A brain abscess is an area inside the brain filled with pus. The abscess often has a skin, called a capsule, surrounding it. A growing abscess is dangerous and produces many of its symptoms by the pressure it exerts on nearby regions of the brain.

Cause: A brain abscess begins when bacteria somehow get into the brain and multiply. Most abscesses begin with an infection in other parts of the body, usually the sinuses, middle ear, teeth, or jaw. Sometimes infections in the chest or lungs travel to the brain, and sometimes a brain abscess results from a wound to the skull.

Noticeable symptoms: Most people with a brain abscess have a headache that does not go away. They may also have mild fever, seizures, nausea, or a stiff neck, usually several together. Depending on the location of the abscess in the brain, speech, movement, or balance may be affected, with symptoms similar to those of a stroke. *A brain abscess is a medical emergency; the patient should get to the emergency room of a hospital as soon as possible.*

Diagnosis: Since many of the symptoms of a brain abscess can have other causes, a physician will ask about recent travel and known infections to eliminate specific diseases that would require a different treatment. After the physician rules out other causes, a CT scan and probably a CT-directed biopsy of the brain (a procedure to remove and examine directly tissue from the brain) will be performed to make a specific diagnosis.

Treatment: Two types of treatment are usually combined. Antibiotics are prescribed to cure the infection, and the abscess is physically removed by a surgical procedure. Often intravenous antibiotics will be administered even before the diagnosis is certain, since halting the infection is vital. After an abscess has been located, a surgeon will cut the abscess out or use aspiration to suck out the diseased material.

The combination treatment is very effective. Approximately 90% of people with a brain abscess survive. Half of the survivors, however, have continuing problems related to the damage the abscess causes to the brain, which may include seizures or personality changes.

Prevention: Prompt treatment of sinus infections, ear infections, and other infections of the face and jaw reduces the risk. Good dental hygiene (flossing and brushing regularly and thoroughly) is important, since a gum abscess may break through to become a brain abscess. People with deep head wounds should use antibiotics to reduce risk. Also, anyone with a heart murmur or a surgical implant (such as an artificial hip) should take antibiotics before undergoing dental work (the dentist will prescribe them if aware of the situation).

Risk factors: About a quarter of all brain abscesses occur in children between ages 2 and 15; the most common ages of onset are between 10 and 35. Males of all ages are twice as likely as females to develop a brain abscess. They are uncommon in elderly people.

Diseases that harm the immune system, such as HIV infection, also increase the risk of a brain abscess.

Breakbone fever

See **Dengue fever**

Breast cancer

DISEASE

TYPE: CANCER

See also
Cancers
Fibrocystic breast disease
Genetic diseases
Hormonal system

Not all breast lumps are cancerous. Most are benign, or noncancerous. But all lumps should be treated with suspicion. Breast cancer can be fatal, but with early detection and treatment most patients survive.

Types: Like other cancers, those that develop in the breast are characterized by the uncontrolled growth and spread of abnormal cells.

There are various types of breast cancer. Noninvasive types are confined to the milk-producing glands and their ducts. Invasive types have spread into the fatty tissue of the breast. There are noninherited forms and inherited forms caused by either the *BRCA1* or *BRCA2* gene. Estrogen, the female hormone, encourages the growth of some tumors, while other tumors are estrogen-negative.

Cause: It is not yet possible to pinpoint the specific causes of breast cancer. However, a variety of factors have been implicated in the disease. It is theorized that two or more factors usually are required to promote development of a tumor. Inheritance of the *BRCA1* or *BRCA2* gene increases susceptibility. Obesity and environmental factors such as radiation and pesticides increase risk as well. Birth control pills, hormone replacement therapy, consumption of alcohol, and diets high in fat may also increase risk. Risk increases with age, perhaps because as people age, they lose some ability to repair damaged DNA molecules. In mice an infectious virus causes breast cancer, and it is possible that a similar virus exists in humans.

Incidence: Each year approximately 194,000 Americans are diagnosed with breast cancer, and about 40,000 die from the disease. The incidence of new cases increased significantly in recent decades, but the death rates declined thanks to early detection and improved treatment. The great majority of breast cancer cases occur in women, but each year about 1,500 cases are diagnosed in men. Inherited forms of breast cancer, which usually strike younger women, account for 5 to 10% of new cases.

Noticeable symptoms: Most breast cancers are found during self-examination. The patient feels or sees a lump in or near the breast or in the underarm area. Other common signs include thickening or distortion of the breast, a discharge from the nipple, and skin irritation or discoloration. A person who experiences such symptoms should see a doctor as soon as possible.

With your hands on your waist, press inward and raise your shoulders. Turn from side to side and look for any differences between breasts, especially sores, nipple changes, or discharge. Raise your hands above your head and repeat the comparison.

A good time to complete the examination is after a bath, running wet, soapy hands along the breasts to feel for any lumps or thickening. This can be started while standing, but a more detailed examination should be completed while lying on your back, preferably with a pillow under the arm below the breast being examined. Move fingers to the nipple first and then away in a circular motion, making sure that the whole breast is covered. Also squeeze and then depress the nipple to watch for discharge and to feel for lumps under it.

Diagnosis: During an examination, a physician will carefully feel the breast for masses and examine the breast surface for any skin changes or other abnormalities. If a suspicious lump

Breast self-examination

About 90% of all breast cancers are found by women themselves. A regular monthly self-examination leads to early detection, important both for safety and for reducing the amount of surgery that might be required in case cancer is detected.

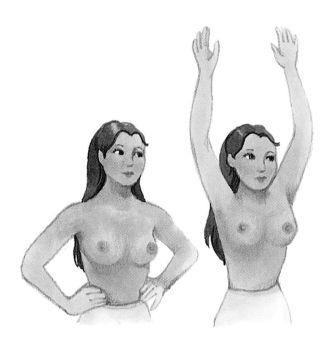

is detected or if a *mammogram* (a low-dose x-ray of the breast) finds an abnormal area, a *biopsy* will be performed. In this procedure a small amount of tissue is removed from the suspect area and examined under a microscope. Cancer cells look markedly different from normal cells. Other tests can determine if the tumor is estrogen-positive and how rapidly the tumor cells are dividing.

Stages and progress: Determining the stage of the cancer is critical for choosing the most effective treatment. Staging describes the size of the tumor and whether it has spread to nearby lymph nodes or to other organs. A widely used staging system assigns a category of I, II, III, or IV. I is an early stage, with no indication that the cancer has spread beyond the breast. IV is the most advanced stage, with the cancer having spread, or *metastasized* (muh-TAAST-uh-SIYZD), to distant sites such as bones or to lymph nodes not near the breast. The more advanced the cancer, the more difficult it is to treat.

Treatment options: The plan of treatment recommended by a physician depends on the stage of the cancer, the patient's general health, and the patient's preferences. Conventional options are surgery, radiation, and chemotherapy. Often all three are used. Surgery may involve the complete removal of the breast in a *mastectomy* (maa-STEHK-tuh-mee). Or only the tumor and nearby tissue may be removed in a *lumpectomy* (luhm-PEHK-tuh-mee). Often a dozen or more lymph nodes under the adjacent arm are removed to determine if the tumor has spread to the nodes.

Radiation therapy, or radiotherapy, uses high-energy x-rays to kill cancer cells. Chemotherapy uses drugs to kill cancer cells. Both radiation and chemotherapy harm normal cells and have unpleasant short-term side effects. Radiation often causes fatigue. Chemotherapy may cause hair loss, nausea, diarrhea, and mouth sores.

Following primary treatment, many breast cancer patients take the drug tamoxifen for five years. Tamoxifen works against tumors sensitive to estrogen and has been shown to lower significantly the risk of breast cancer recurrence.

Prevention and early detection: Various practices have been suggested as being helpful in reducing the risk of breast cancer. These include regular exercise, a low-fat diet, and avoidance of alcohol and tobacco. Although such practices are beneficial to general health, there is no definitive evidence that they protect against breast cancer.

In contrast, many studies, although not all, support the importance of early detection of tumors in saving lives. The best tool for early detection is the mammogram. This x-ray picture of the breast can find tumors up to two years or more before they are large enough to be felt. The American Cancer Society recommends that women age 40 and older have an annual mammogram and an annual breast examination by a health care professional. All women age 20 and older should examine their own breasts once a month.

| **Bright's disease** | *See* **Kidney diseases** |
| **Broken bones** | *See* **Fractures, strains, and sprains** |

Bronchitis

(brong-KIY-tihs)

DISEASE

TYPE: INFECTIOUS (VIRAL)
OR ENVIRONMENTAL

See also
Asthma
Common cold
COPD
(chronic obstructive
pulmonary disease)
Coughs
Cystic fibrosis
Emphysema
Environment and disease
Lungs
Measles (rubeola)
Nose and throat conditions
Pertussis
Tobacco and disease
Viruses and disease

Don't smoke   Avoid aspirin

Young children who have recently had a bad cold or older people who have smoked tobacco for many years are most likely to experience an attack of a lung and throat disorder called bronchitis. Others may develop infections that attack the bronchial tubes that also are termed bronchitis.

Cause: *Acute infectious bronchitis* is caused by a viral infection of the bronchi (BRONG-kiy)—the air passages that lead from the throat to the lungs. *Chronic bronchitis* is more often environmental, occurring when the bronchi are repeatedly irritated by tobacco smoke or air pollution.

Acute infectious bronchitis is most likely to occur in winter and in children after a viral disease such as a cold, measles, or whooping cough. Active or passive cigarette smoking, air pollution, lung infections, or abnormal growth of the bronchi are the main causes of chronic bronchitis in adults. Chronic bronchitis usually accompanies emphysema, a serious lung disease of the air sacs.

Incidence: As many as 1 adult in 20 may have chronic bronchitis. It is especially common in smokers over 40 years of age.

Noticeable symptoms: Symptoms of both acute and chronic bronchitis include a cough that releases mucous secretions from the lungs called *sputum* (SPYOO-tuhm), breathlessness or wheezing, fever, chest pain upon coughing, soreness, and back pain.

Diagnosis: A physician will listen with a stethoscope for abnormal sounds, called rales (RAHLZ), from the lungs as a breath is taken. Chest x-rays give the physician a more accurate determination of the affected airways and can be used to rule out other lung diseases. A lung test (blowing into a tube) measures lung capacity. For chronic bronchitis a blood test can measure oxygen in the blood.

Treatment options: Treatment for both acute and chronic bronchitis attacks includes bed rest, lots of fluids, medication to reduce fever, antibiotics if a secondary bacterial infection attacks the lungs, and nebulizers to help remove mucus from airways. Expectorant cough medicines, not suppressants, are recommended for treating the characteristic bronchitis cough. Aspirin is not recommended for reducing fever in young people because its use can induce *Reye's syndrome.*

Prevention: The safest course of action is to avoid smoking and breathing polluted air, smoke, dust, or fumes. Cold or damp environments also contribute to the disease. Eating a well-balanced diet, drinking enough fluids, and staying away from people who have viral infections also help.

| Brucellosis | *See* **Animal diseases and humans** |
| Bruises | *See* **Bleeding and bruises** |

Bruxism
(BRUK-sihz-uhm)

SYMPTOM

TYPE: MECHANICAL;
     MENTAL

See also
Dental illnesses and conditions
Teeth

Practice meditation

Bruxism is the grinding or clenching of teeth. It is an unintentional, subconscious behavior, occurring most often while the person sleeps. Many people with bruxism are unaware of the problem until someone else points it out or until they see the physical damage caused by the habit.

Parts affected: Clenching the jaws together and grinding the lower teeth against the upper teeth causes excessive wear on the teeth. The teeth and fillings may be chipped, broken, or loosened. As the tooth enamel is ground off, the teeth become sensitive to cold, pressure, and other stimuli. Lack of enamel also leads to tooth decay. Receding gums may occur, and in extreme cases the teeth are worn down to stumps. The grinder also may experience headaches, earaches, hearing loss, and sore facial muscles.

Cause: A variety of factors may trigger or exacerbate bruxism. These include emotional stress and nervous tension, smoking, alcohol, antidepressant drugs, vitamin or mineral deficiencies, tooth fillings and other dental procedures, and mouth injuries. Young children may grind their teeth in response to the discomfort of ailments such as colds, allergies, and ear infections.

Treatment options: Bruxism is most common in children. Fortunately, juvenile bruxism usually disappears spontaneously. Treatment is needed only when the habit persists.

When a dentist sees signs of bruxism, the patient's medical history and habits are reviewed. Patients are advised to reduce stress, perhaps by trying psychotherapy or yoga, and

Avoid alcohol

Don't smoke

to eliminate use of alcohol and tobacco. If an antidepressant is a suspected cause, reducing the dose or switching to another antidepressant may be recommended.

The dentist helps the patient learn how to position the teeth and tongue properly. If necessary, a customized mouth guard is made to be worn while sleeping. The mouth guard absorbs the punishment that would otherwise be endured by the teeth, thereby reducing further damage to the teeth.

Bubonic plague	*See* **Plague**
Buerger's disease	*See* **Circulatory system; Veins**

Bulimia
(boo-LIHM-ee-uh)

DISEASE

TYPE: EATING DISORDER

See also
Anorexia nervosa
Constipation
Diet and disease
Hemorrhoids
Nausea
Obesity

Bulimia, or *bulimia nervosa,* is a serious eating disorder characterized by episodes of binge eating alternating with self-induced vomiting, purging (using laxatives to promote bowel evacuation), excessive exercising, or a combination of those behaviors. The purpose of the vomiting, purging, and exercise is to avoid the weight gain induced by binging. Like the eating disorder anorexia nervosa, which is characterized by reducing food intake to tiny amounts, bulimia most often occurs in teenage girls and young women. People experiencing bulimia typically have distorted self-images and other deep-seated psychological problems. The word *bulimic* is sometimes used to describe a person with bulimia.

Cause: Doctors do not know why some people develop the eating disorder bulimia, but family pressures and profound psychological problems are thought to play a role. Like people with anorexia nervosa, those with bulimia tend to have parents who are achievement oriented and controlling. Diet and slimness often are important topics of family conversation and so figure in the patient's sense of self-esteem.

Those with bulimia frequently have a history of being overweight. Thus bulimia may be viewed as a form of overcompensation. People with bulimia also tend to be somewhat older than those with anorexia and more frequently exhibit antisocial and compulsive behavior patterns along with their eating disorder.

One of the key signs of bulimia is the food binge—eating a large amount of a high-calorie food in a short period of time. This is frequently followed by vomiting or purging along with feelings of guilt for the behavior that may lead to a period of self-imposed fasting. But after a time the feelings subside, and another binge is started.

Incidence: Bulimia is more difficult to detect than anorexia, though, like anorexia, it usually occurs in young females from middle- or upper-class families. Bulimia is believed to be more common than anorexia and may affect up to 19% of college-age women. Reports of incidence vary widely though, and some claim percentages as low as 3% of young women. Those with anorexia sometimes also exhibit the bulimic's binge-purge behavior.

In addition to young women, ballet dancers, gymnasts, jockeys, and wrestlers also are vulnerable to bulimia. People with these professions or hobbies need to keep their weight low to be successful; but instead of maintaining a regular regimen of dieting and exercise, the performer or athlete with bulimia loses control of diet and then overcompensates in a harmful way, either by purging, fasting, or overexercising. Most male bulimics do not purge.

Noticeable symptoms: Anorexia eventually becomes obvious because the patient becomes extremely emaciated. Weight changes caused by bulimia are subtler and therefore harder to detect. Though bulimics may rapidly gain or lose, they usually remain within 20% of their normal weight.

The clearest symptom of bulimia is the eating binge, although an observer would get to see this only by chance. People with bulimia nearly always gorge themselves secretly. High-calorie foods tend to be favored for binges. Some people with bulimia embark on several different eating binges each day for several days at a time before purging themselves with laxatives or with self-induced vomiting. Medicines called *diuretics* (DIY-uh-REHT-ihks) may be used to promote urination and thus temporarily lower weight through loss of fluids. A period of self-imposed starvation or excessive exercise may follow an episode of binging.

Diagnosis: A doctor will want to make certain that the suspected disorder is bulimia and not another recently recognized eating problem, *binge eating disorder.* Binge eating, which is more common than bulimia, involves eating abnormal amounts of food and leads to significant weight gain. Low self-esteem and depression are among the possible causes. Binge eating is not accompanied by frantic attempts to undo the excess intake.

The periodic binging and purging of a person with bulimia eventually affect the patient's body in a variety of ways. Stomach acid passes through the mouth during repeated vomiting, leaving teeth sharp and rough. Acid also irritates and inflames the esophagus and pharynx, giving the bulimic a puffy-cheeked appearance. Laxative abuse often causes hemorrhoids and chronic constipation by upsetting normal rhythms of the digestive tract. Vomiting can cause dehydration and electrolyte imbalances, as can diuretic and laxative abuse. But unlike women with anorexia, bulimic women do not lose their periods because they usually remain close to their normal body weight.

Treatment options: Early diagnosis and treatment of bulimia are important because the longer the disorder continues, the more difficult treatment becomes. Bulimics can be treated on an outpatient basis to help them restore control over eating habits. A doctor may prescribe an antidepressant such as fluoxetine and may have the patient take part in individual and group therapy. This can allow the bulimic to begin confronting the underlying personal and family problems that helped bring on the disorder.

Even though patients show clear signs of progress in dealing with their eating and emotional problems, psychiatric counseling and physical checkups often continue on a regular basis for months or longer. About 74% of bulimics recover fully with treatment, and 99% achieve at least partial recovery.

Stages and progress: Bulimia usually begins with dieting to lose weight. But some girls and young women lose control over the craving for food that dieting brings and suddenly eat large amounts of high-calorie foods in a matter of hours. Following this, or after other similar binges, the binger suffers guilt and self-recrimination for having lost control, combined with the fear of becoming overweight. Then purging, perhaps with the use of diuretics, and self-induced vomiting begin. A period of self-inflicted starvation or extreme dieting often follows until the next episode of binge eating.

Those with bulimia generally do not suffer the severe physical effects that those with anorexia do, and death from bulimia is rare. Frequent purging can cause heart damage, however, and acid in the throat may contribute to later development of cancer.

Breaking the binge-purge cycle can be difficult, especially if underlying psychological problems are severe.

Burns and scalds

DISEASE

TYPE: INJURY

See also
Blister
Gangrene
Hypothermia
Shock
Sunburn

Phone doctor

Most people burn themselves sooner or later; however, most burns are minor and heal naturally.

Cause: Burns are caused by contact with high heat or flames, electricity, chemicals, or exposure to the sun. Scalds are burns caused by contact with hot liquids or steam.

Incidence: It is estimated that more than a million burns or scalds require medical attention annually in the United States alone. About 50,000 of these burns or scalds cause the victim to be hospitalized, half in special burn-treatment units. Each year about 4,500 Americans die from burns or scalds directly, while lowered immune defense caused by burns or scalds contributes to pneumonia or other infections that lead to somewhat more than that number of deaths.

Noticeable symptoms: Burns are classified according to their degree of seriousness.

- *First-degree burns* are the least serious. They are often caused by contact with hot objects or scalding. Symptoms include redness, mild swelling, and pain. These burns usually heal by themselves. Most sunburns are first-degree burns.
- *Second-degree burns* are often caused by direct contact with very hot liquids. They can also result from contact with gasoline, kerosene, and chemicals. Symptoms of second-degree burns include red or blotchy skin, blisters, and swelling. Second-degree burns are noticeably wet. This wetness results when plasma, the liquid part of blood, seeps out through the damaged skin layers. Severe sunburns are second-degree burns.
- *Third-degree burns* occur when the heat is at a high temperature or the contact is long. They might result from direct contact with flames, chemicals, or electricity, or from immersion in hot water. With third-degree burns all skin layers are destroyed, resulting in a charred grayish appearance. A person with a third-degree burn will not feel pain because the nerve endings have been destroyed.

Diagnosis: Your physician will note the extent of damage to skin, fat, and muscle. He or she will also look for symptoms of dehydration and for infections that may occur as a result of the burns.

Simple safety habits can prevent most burns from happening in the first place.

Treatment options: The type of treatment needed depends on four things: (1) the seriousness of the burn, (2) the amount of the body burned, (3) the parts of the body burned, and (4) the substance that caused the burn. These are detailed in the table at the bottom of the page.

Minor burns usually do not need medical attention, but first-aid steps as outlined on the next page are helpful. More serious second-degree burns and all third-degree burns must be treated by a physician. First aid should be applied immediately, however, without waiting for the physician.

The physician's treatment will depend on the type of burn and its severity. Treatment may include replacing lost liquids, either orally or intravenously, and therapy for shock. The doctor may prescribe antibiotics or an antibacterial ointment. In cases of severe burning hospitalization may be required. For the most serious third-degree burns skin grafts may be necessary.

Prevention: The best way to prevent burns is to avoid the type of accidents that lead to burns. Make sure that electrical appliances are cared for and used properly. Avoid chemical burns by carefully following instructions on products that contain potentially dangerous substances. Wear protective gear such as gloves and eye goggles when handling chemicals. Avoid keeping flammable materials such as gasoline or paint thinners at home, but always have smoke alarms and fire extinguishers in the home.

Degrees of Burn Danger

Type	Degree	Extent of Burn and Body Parts Burned
Minor	All first-degree and some second-degree burns	Less than 15%* of the body for adults and less than 10% for children and the elderly
Severe	Most second-degree burns	10 to 25% of the body for adults and 10 to 20% for children and the elderly; electrical burns are also termed severe
Critical	Some second-degree and all third-degree burns	More than 25% of the body for adults and more than 20% for children and the elderly; second- or third-degree burns of face, hands, eyes, or feet

*One percent of the body is about the size of the victim's open hand.

Bursitis

(bur-SIY-tuhs)

DISEASE

TYPE: MECHANICAL;
      INFECTION
      (BACTERIAL)

See also
Gout
Inflammation
Rheumatoid arthritis
"Staph"
Tennis elbow and related problems

The body has 156 fluid-filled sacs, or bursas; most are located in joints, where they act as cushions to minimize friction. An inflammation of a bursa is called bursitis.

Parts affected: Any bursa may become inflamed. Joints that are particularly susceptible to bursitis include those in the shoulder, elbow, hip, knee, ankle, and big toe.

Cause: Bursitis is usually caused by excessive trauma. It typically results from an injury or from a repeated physical activity. Bursitis may be precipitated by certain types of arthritis, such as rheumatoid arthritis, or gout. It also may result from infection, usually by the bacterium *Staphylococcus aureus*.

Noticeable symptoms: Bursitis is often accompanied by pain, redness, and swelling of the area around the inflamed bursa. One's ability to move the joint may be limited.

Associations: Bursitis in the shoulder is the most common form, but bursas become sore at other locations as well. One cause of "tennis elbow" is an inflammation of the bursa that develops when the elbow is overused (inflammation of the tendons in that joint is also called tennis elbow). "Housemaid's knee" is an inflammation of the bursa at the front of the knee that results from excessive kneeling. "Weaver's bottom," an inflammation of a bursa in the hip area, is caused by prolonged sitting on hard surfaces. Continued pressure on a bunion (a thickening of the joint at the base of the big toe), perhaps from tight-fitting shoes, can cause bursitis.

Stages and progress: Bursitis often clears up within a week, particularly if the aggravating condition is avoided, and the inflamed joint is rested. However, if you have recently injured a joint or if the pain is severe or lasts more than one week, it is advisable to see a doctor.

Treatment options: Common anti-inflammatory drugs such as aspirin or ibuprofen often relieve pain and swelling. In severe cases a physician may inject a corticosteroid medication into the affected area. The doctor will usually suggest exercises to help prevent the formation of scar tissue. If a bursa becomes infected or if it is subject to repeated inflammations, surgery may be necessary.

Caisson disease	*See* **Bends**

Calluses and corns	*See* **Foot problems**

Cancers

DISEASE

TYPE: GENETIC; ENVIRONMENTAL; VIRAL

A generation or two ago the word *cancer* was avoided in polite conversation. The diseases collectively known as cancer seemed at that time too horrible and too surely fatal to discuss. Changes in society, increases in the incidence of many cancers, new treatment successes, and a better understanding of disease have since changed the way people talk about the second leading cause of death in the United States (after heart disease).

Cause: Cancer begins as a disorder of the genetic material DNA (deoxyribonucleic acid), the large molecule that is composed of genes that direct development and activity at the cellular level. Although thought of primarily in terms of heredity, the day-to-day function of DNA is to direct the production of the proteins that carry out all operations of each cell. Defects in DNA that cause cells to proliferate, either as solid masses (tumors) of one kind of cell throughout the body or as large numbers of cells in the blood, are called cancers—although if a tumor neither spreads to other locations in the body nor encroaches on neighboring tissues except by pressure, it is "benign" instead of "malignant." Cancers are also classed by the type of tissue in which they originate—*carcinomas* (KAHR-suh-NOH-muhz) in the inner or outer linings of organs; *sarcomas* (sahr-KOH-muhz) in muscle or bone; *leukemias* (loo-KEE-mee-uhz) in blood-forming cells; and *lymphomas* (lihm-FOH-muhz) in lymph tissue.

Genes involved in cancer are of two main types: Some encourage cell growth; others do just the opposite. Many cancers involve defects in genes that control cell division or that destroy cells recognized as defective. In nearly all cancers more than one gene must be damaged for the cells to reproduce and spread. Because such a combination is needed, cancers develop in stages. In the earlier stage some DNA is defective, but the genes involved cannot greatly affect cell growth on their own. Later, another gene is damaged by something in the environment or perhaps just in the course of normal cell division. The combination of two (or more) "bad" genes sets off growth of cancerous cells.

Often the media report that a "cancer gene" has been discovered. This means that the gene is one that can occur in a form that, when combined with one or more other genes, produces cancer. Almost all genes come in several different forms. For example, one "breast cancer gene" produces growth of tissue in the breast; but after the tissue is in place, other genes normally turn the "breast cancer gene" off. Some forms of this "breast cancer gene" are harder to turn off than others or produce more rapid growth than others. When other genes that normally turn off the "breast-cancer gene" become damaged, the "breast cancer gene" continues to tell cells to grow, resulting in cancer, especially if the "breast cancer gene" is a form that produces rapid growth.

Sometimes a person is born with a gene that does not function correctly, while in other instances a gene may become damaged. There are many ways that DNA can be damaged. Chemicals in the environment are a frequent cause, especially the chemicals in "tar" from burning tobacco. Viruses, which manipulate DNA to reproduce, can also initiate cancer. Radiation, including radioactivity and ultraviolet rays in sunlight, may damage DNA. Often the specific cause of a cancer is not known. Cancer growth can be promoted by undamaged genes whose normal operation is controlled by another gene that is now failing to function properly.

Incidence: Somewhat more than half a million Americans die from cancer as a primary cause each year. While this is still only slightly more than two-thirds as many as die from heart disease, heart disease deaths have declined dramatically in past decades, and cancer deaths have declined only slightly more than 1% since 1990. This decline would be much greater, however, if it were not for the increasing age of the population, since most incidence of cancer rises with age.

In 2000 about 1.2 million new cancer cases were diagnosed, and about 552,200 persons died, nearly all from cancers diagnosed in previous years.

The greatest rise in the number of cancer deaths is from lung cancer. Lung cancer accounts for more than a quarter of all cancer deaths in the United States. However, lung cancer is not the only form of cancer for which death rates are rising. Increases in death rates have occurred in a number of cancer types, including melanomas, liver cancer, multiple myeloma, prostate cancer, non-Hodgkin's lymphoma, and cancers of the esophagus, kidney, breast, and brain.

The greatest concern is lung cancer in women, which has doubled since the U.S. "war on cancer" began in 1973, almost certainly because many more women than previously began to use cigarettes between 1920 and 1950. Another significant increase in incidence is for the skin cancer melanoma. Since the 1930s the increase has been from 1 in 1,500 persons to 1 in 1,200 persons. This increase is thought to be connected to exposure to sunlight, although that is difficult to prove for a large population—the relationship seems clearer in individual cases. Since the rate change seems too high to be accounted for by sunbathing alone, especially since fewer people now work outdoors, perhaps changes in the ozone layer or another environmental factor is involved. A third cancer that has risen greatly in incidence affects men only; prostate cancer has risen at about the same rate as has melanoma. The reason for such a rise is not completely clear.

Cancer in children is also rising in incidence, especially acute lymphocytic leukemia and brain or nervous system cancers.

Noticeable symptoms: Many changes occur with cancers. Cancers often form lumps or sores that can be felt or seen. Bleeding is a common symptom, as is unexplained pain. There may be otherwise unexplained symptoms of weight loss, nausea, or changes in bowel movements or stools. Sometimes persistent flulike symptoms occur as the immune system attempts to fight the disease. ***When in doubt, consult a physician.***

Diagnosis: Although a physician can often recognize cancer from experience or from viewing a sore, a sonogram, or an x-ray image, the main proof comes from *biopsy*, the direct examination of cells by a trained specialist called a *pathologist* (paa-THOL-uh-jihst). Cancer cells removed from a lump (*tumor*), or in some cases from blood or other tissue, are examined under a microscope for characteristic changes. Depending on the location of the possible cancer, a tissue sample for a biopsy may be taken in a physician's office with little discomfort or may require surgery in a hospital setting.

Stages and progress: Cancer is thought to begin with a single cell. The cell becomes a cancer when it and its daughter cells begin to divide rapidly. Solid tumors grow over organs and invade neighboring organs, interfering with their function, or cancerous blood cells begin to replace normal cells in the blood. The greatest danger from solid tumors comes when cells break away and lodge in other parts of the body. In that case the cancer is said to spread, or *metastasize* (muh-TAAST-uh-sɪʏz). With many cancer sites throughout the body the disease becomes much more difficult to treat.

Treatment options: From ancient times medical practitioners have treated cancers by removing tumors with surgery. This approach is usually successful if the cancer has not taken over an organ needed for life or metastasized, but for many cancers surgery comes too late. Ionizing radiation (dis-

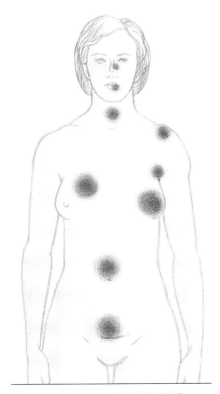

CANCER'S WARNING SIGNS

C hange in bowel or bladder habits

A sore that does not heal

U nusual bleeding or discharge

T hickening or lump in breast or elsewhere

I ndigestion or difficulty swallowing

O bvious change in a wart or mole

N agging cough or hoarseness

covered at the end of the nineteenth century), from x- rays or more often today from radioactive materials, kills cancer cells somewhat faster than it does normal cells. Thus radiation can treat cancers that are not treatable by surgery.

For the past few decades therapy with chemicals that interfere with cell division or otherwise have a greater effect on cancers than on normal cells has been available. This approach, called *chemotherapy* (kee-moh-THEHR-uh-pee), has been responsible for the main successes of the modern era, producing high cure rates for some cancers and improved cure rates for many others. ("Cure" in cancer is difficult to establish. Generally, physicians treat a five-year period free of symptoms as a cure.) In recent years new classes of drug treatments have been successful in treating specific cancers by interfering with specific signals that cells use between them. More than half of signaling chemicals can contribute to cancer formation or spread. The first drugs to interfere with cell signaling were Herceptin, for breast cancer, and Gleevec, for certain varieties of leukemia and gastrointestinal cancer. Another successful approach has been to introduce a virus programmed to grow in and destroy cells that have specific genetic damage, but nowhere else.

A recent approach that has seen some success is to enlist parts of the patient's immune system to attack the cancer. White blood cells are "trained" outside the body to produce an immune response to the cancer cells, then reintroduced into the patient's bloodstream.

Surgery in the past often involved removal of large body parts and organs. Today doctors try to remove the minimum necessary to get rid of the disease. For example, breast cancer is not the only cancer for which lumpectomy is replacing a radical operation. In the early 1980s bladder cancer was treated by removal of the bladder, with a consequent need for an artificial bag to collect urine. But bladder lumpectomy combined with chemotherapy and radiation was shown in the 1990s to be as effective as removal of the bladder.

Research has shown that during and after treatment, membership in self-help support groups increases survival rates. One study of breast cancer showed that people who took part in support sessions lived twice as long as matched

12-Step meeting

members of a control group—three years after diagnosis as opposed to a year and a half for the control group.

Prevention and risk factors: Cancer is caused by genes, but it is usually not a purely hereditary disease. Even when genetic heritage predisposes a person to a particular kind of cancer, some other event is usually required to produce the tumor. Often that other event is something in the environment—a chemical, radiation, or a virus, for example. In other cases simple aging may cause humans to lose some ability to repair damaged DNA. When the damage is repaired, no cancer results, but older people have less of the enzyme that is needed for such repair.

One rough estimate of the relative roles of causative factors is as follows:

Chemicals that naturally occur in foods	35
Tobacco	30
Sex and reproductive history	7
Occupational hazards, mainly chemical	4
Alcoholic beverages	3
Food additives	1

*The percentages for these possible causes do not add up to 100 because the causes of most instances of cancer are unknown.

Food: The media have recently pointed to fat as a cancer villain, but hundreds of other substances or chemicals in food are suspected as cancer promoters as well. Only a few, such as chemicals from the aflatoxin molds that infect grains and peanuts, have been proven to cause cancer. The National Cancer Institute, however, estimates that more than a third of cancers may be caused in part by diet.

While most diet concerns revolve around eating too much of a dangerous chemical, people also have come to believe that ingesting more of certain chemicals can prevent cancer. These include vitamins such as C or E. The mineral selenium is also suspected of helping to ward off cancer. These possibilities are based on statistical analyses but are not completely established.

Don't smoke

Avoid alcohol

The best correlation is between high intake of vitamin E and lowered risk of cancer.

Tobacco and alcohol: The main known cause of preventable cancer is smoking or chewing tobacco, which causes several types of cancer. Stopping smoking is the main decision to be made in cancer prevention. Heavy drinking of alcoholic beverages is also known to induce cancer of the mouth, esophagus, pancreas, and liver.

Sex: Some cancers are associated with the act of sex in one way or another; for example, genital warts spread sexually can become malignant. Noticeable variations in cancer risk associated with reproductive history are largely statistical, with actual causes unexplained. Women who have had children have a lower risk of ovarian cancer, for example, but the reason is unknown.

Occupation: The role of occupational exposure to chemicals in the causing of cancer receives a great deal of media attention, in part because workers who think their cancer is job-related tend to sue the companies involved. It is difficult, however, to prove job-related cancers except in the most clear-cut instances, such as asbestos-caused lung cancer. Dioxins have long been known to cause cancer in animals, for example, but good evidence that these chemicals, which contaminate pesticides and are produced by burning, cause cancer in humans is hard to find. Farmers have higher cancer rates than the rest of the population, and pesticides are suspected. Other chemicals used in such industries as manufacturing of computer chips are suspected as well.

Farmers are among the persons with high rates of melanoma. This deadly cancer seems to occur most often in people who are exposed to ultraviolet radiation from the sun. Good sunscreens are thought to help protect against melanoma.

Radiation: Radiation from x-rays or radioactive elements is so powerful a cause of cancer that most workers with heavy exposure to radiation develop the disease. Steps are taken today to reduce exposure to x-rays and other obvious sources of radioactive elements. Radon, however, is a colorless, odorless radioactive gas that escapes from granite or other rocks. It may enter people's homes through the basement. Radon can contribute to lung cancer unless air in affected basements is exchanged with outside air on a regular basis.

Stay out of sun

Another form of radiation—electromagnetic fields, especially from high-voltage, long-distance transmission lines—is also thought by some to cause cancer. This contention has been rejected by most experts in magnetism, but it still has many believers.

Germs: In some cases infections are known to be a causative agent; thus these forms of cancer can be prevented by vaccination or effective treatment. Liver cancer, for example, can be induced by hepatitis B, but there is a vaccine available that prevents the original disease from developing. The bacterium *Helicobacter pylori*, now known to be the chief cause of stomach and duodenal ulcers, is also implicated in stomach cancer. Known cases of infection with this bacteria can be cured with antibiotics. Since both liver and stomach cancer have exceptionally low survival rates, preventing their occurrence in the first place is a first line of prevention.

Water: The list of potential causes of cancer is so long that some say "even drinking water causes cancer" to ridicule fears. But drinking water does cause cancer! Chlorinated water raises the risk for rectal and bladder cancers about 21 to 38%, although the risks of infection from untreated water are far greater than the added cancer burden.

Candidiasis

(KAAN-dih-DIY-uh-sihs)

DISEASE

TYPE: FUNGAL INFECTION

See also
Fungus diseases

Candidiasis is mainly a fungal infection of the skin and mucous membranes. Typical sites include the mouth and throat (*thrush*) and the female vagina (*vaginal yeast infection*). Much less common is *invasive candidiasis,* in which the infection enters the bloodstream, threatening damage to the liver, kidneys, or other internal organs.

Cause: Candidiasis is caused by a single-celled yeast called *Candida.* The yeast cells are ubiquitous—present everywhere—and ordinarily the body keeps their numbers under control. They cannot, for example, reproduce well on dry skin. On the moist mucous membranes bacteria keep them in check. The immune system also attacks them.

Under certain circumstances, however, the yeast organisms may reproduce out of control. When babies aren't kept dry between diaper changes, colonies grow on the moist skin. When antibiotics are used to fight bacterial infections, they may also kill off the useful bacteria on the mucous membranes. Also, any disorder that weakens the immune system reduces protection against the yeast.

Incidence: Because the yeast is naturally widespread, infections are very common.

Noticeable symptoms: The skin or mucous membranes are irritated by the spreading yeast colonies and become inflamed—red, itchy, and sore. If the infection occurs in the mouth, milky white patches of the yeast may be visible. A vaginal infection may produce a thick, whitish discharge. Itching in moist folds of the body, such as between the scrotum and thigh in men, is another symptom.

Diagnosis: Samples of the yeast cells can be identified under a microscope. If *Candida* invades the esophagus, it is diagnosed using an endoscope, a tube passed down the throat.

Treatment options: Candidiasis is successfully treated with antifungal medicines, either applied *topically* (on the surface) or taken internally.

Risk factors: People who have to undergo extended treatment with antibiotics or corticosteroids are at higher than usual risk. So are pregnant women and diabetics; men with diabetes may develop a *Candida* infection under the foreskin of the penis. People with damaged immune systems (such as those with AIDS or those receiving cancer treatment) are especially susceptible.

Canker

DISEASE

TYPE: UNKNOWN

See also
Cold sore

A small sore in the mouth that develops rapidly but usually heals without treatment may be a canker, or *aphthous* (AAF-thuhs) *ulcer*. Cankers resemble cold sores; however, unlike cold sores, cankers are not contagious.

Cause: Cankers are very common, but their cause is unknown. A number of infectious agents, including viruses and bacteria, have been implicated. There is some evidence that cankers are an autoimmune disorder related to a reaction to one's own immune system. Also, heredity may be involved, with some people predisposed to developing cankers. Various factors seem to trigger outbreaks, including stress, food allergies, nutritional deficiencies, and hormone changes related to menstruation.

Noticeable symptoms: Cankers may occur singly or in clusters. They develop in the fleshy lining of the mouth and on the tongue. A canker typically is less than 0.08 inch in diameter, but may be ten times that size. It resembles a tiny crater, having a yellow or whitish gray center enclosed within a narrow red ring. For about a week the canker stings, especially when one eats or drinks. Then, as the sore begins to heal, the pain lessens. Most cankers heal within two weeks.

Treatment options: Cankers usually heal by themselves. Pain can be relieved by rinsing the mouth several times a day with an antiseptic mouthwash or warm salt water. Both prescription and nonprescription ointments are available to numb the pain; these can be applied to the canker with a cotton swab. If cankers recur frequently or if sores do not heal within three weeks, see a doctor. He or she will examine the mouth for punctures or other injuries. The doctor may recommend blood tests or a biopsy of a sore to determine if there is an underlying cause that requires attention.

Capillaries

(KAAP-uh-LEHR-eez)

The capillaries are tiny blood vessels that deliver fresh blood directly to cells and that remove waste products from the cells. If you think of the circulatory system as being to the body as a water supply and sewers are to a city, then the capillaries are the plumbing pipes in individual kitchens and bathrooms.

Size: The walls of capillaries are only one cell thick, and the cells are flattened like pizzas. A molecule can easily pass from one side of such a cell to the other, conducted through the cell membranes by special protein complexes that project through the membranes and provide passageways.

The smallest capillaries are only three-thousandths of an inch in diameter. Red blood cells, which collect and release oxygen, must pass through the tubes in single file.

Role: Oxygen from blood escapes through capillary walls into body tissues, replaced in the blood by carbon dioxide from the tissues. Water molecules can also penetrate to some degree, along with small molecules dissolved in the blood fluid. As a result, the space around cells is bathed in fluid. Blood pressure maintains a balance between this fluid and the plasma in the capillaries, but there is nearly three times as much fluid outside the circulatory system as in blood. Excess fluid is carried away by the lymphatic system.

The fluid that escapes from the capillaries provides a route for the cells of the immune system to travel to other body cells. Thus, when bacteria or viruses invade cells, the immune system can bring up its army and attack. White blood cells, such as phagocytes and other leukocytes, pass through capillaries' thin walls. (Red blood cells have no passage out of the circulatory system in a healthy body.)

Conditions that affect the capillaries: In hemorrhagic fevers capillaries break and cause bleeding. The red nose of the chronic alcohol abuser stems from a thinning of the capillaries caused by excessive drinking. In a condition called *diabetic retinopathy* (REHT-uhn-AHP-uh-thee) capillaries in the retina may break. This can lead to visual impairment or blindness if not controlled.

Carbuncle	*See* **Boils**
Cardiac	*See* **Heart; Heart attack; Heart failure**

Cardiac muscle

BODY SYSTEM

See also
Alcoholism
Angina
Arrhythmias
Chest pain
Circulatory system
Congenital heart conditions
Diphtheria
Heart
Heart attack
Heart failure
Hypertrophy
Myocarditis
Palpitations
Skeletal muscles
Smooth muscles

The regular beat of the heart about once a second or faster continues throughout a person's life, amounting to more than 2 billion contractions. This heartbeat is among the remarkable feats of the body. A special kind of muscle is needed to accomplish this feat.

Size and location: The muscle tissue of the heart is a special type called cardiac muscle. Its fibers are striped, resembling skeletal muscle. But the stripes in cardiac muscle are bridges that connect one fiber to the next. These bridges account for the involuntary way the heart works, resembling smooth muscle in operating with no conscious control. However, cardiac muscle continues to beat with no outside control, conscious or unconscious. The regular muscle contractions go on even if a section of the heart is removed and kept alive for a time. The bridges are the key to this because they keep adjacent muscle cells beating together.

Role: The heart is one of the main mechanical parts of the body, with the cardiac muscle doing the work of pumping blood through the circulatory system.

Conditions that affect cardiac muscle: Because of its constant activity cardiac muscle requires a steady supply of oxygen to burn glucose for energy. Angina is pain registered by heart muscle that is receiving too little oxygen. Nitroglycerin used to relieve angina apparently works by increasing the supply of the compound nitric oxide in heart muscle, which promotes relaxation. More serious problems arise when oxygen is cut off for even a short time by a blood clot, perhaps the most common type of heart attack.

Inflammation of the heart muscle, or myocarditis (MIY-oh-kahr-DIY-tis), can result from any of several infectious diseases, but especially as a side effect of diphtheria or AIDS. It can also be induced by radiation and cocaine abuse as well as sometimes being a side effect of prescription drugs.

The general name for damage to cardiac muscle is *cardiomyopathy* (KAHR-dee-oh-miy-OP-uh-thee). There are several kinds of damage. Active alcoholism damages heart muscle either as a direct effect of alcohol abuse or through B-vitamin deficiency. Vitamin B_1 deficiency by itself can also cause cardiomyopathy. High blood pressure may affect heart muscle as well. Furthermore, in some individuals the cardiac muscle degenerates for reasons that are unknown at the present time.

An enlarged heart, called *cardiac hypertrophy*, can develop when cardiac muscle increases in bulk because pumping is insufficient. The enlarged heart can produce pressure on nearby organs such as the lungs and often does not succeed in better pumping despite its increased size.

Cardiomyopathy	*See* **Cardiac muscle; Heart failure**
Caries, dental	*See* **Tooth decay**

Carpal tunnel syndrome

INJURY

TYPE: MECHANICAL

See also
Cartilage
Ligaments
Nerves
Tennis elbow and related problems

Most people who get carpal tunnel syndrome have jobs or hobbies that involve repetitive motion of the hand, wrist, or arm.

Cause: Repeating the same hand, wrist, or arm movements hour after hour, day after day is the primary cause of carpal tunnel syndrome. When force is used at the same time, carpal tunnel syndrome becomes even more likely.

The carpal tunnel is a space formed by bones called carpals at the base of the palm and the ligament that covers them. Tendons and an important nerve pass from the forearm into the hand through this narrow space. The position of the hand and wrist determines the amount of pressure on the tendons and nerve. The least pressure occurs when hand and wrist are level; it increases when the hand is bent up or down. Carpal tunnel syndrome develops when repeated motions inflame tendons in the wrist. The tendons swell and put pressure on the nerve, reducing its ability to carry signals to and from the hand.

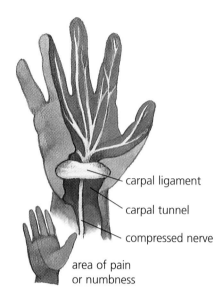

carpal ligament

carpal tunnel

compressed nerve

area of pain
or numbness

Carpal tunnel syndrome occurs when swelling in the tunnel harms the nerve that passes through it.

Incidence: Carpal tunnel syndrome often occurs among workers who have jobs that involve repetitive lifting or finger and wrist motions. People who work with computers are likely candidates. Carpal tunnel syndrome also occurs among amateur and professional musicians, people who do needlework or other crafts involving the fingers and wrists, food-service workers who chop and cut, and athletes in certain sports.

Women who are pregnant, are taking birth control pills (oral contraceptives), or are in menopause (the life stage when they stop menstruating) are more prone to get carpal tunnel syndrome. Conditions such as diabetes, thyroid disease, rheumatoid arthritis, and Lyme disease have also been linked to carpal tunnel syndrome. In addition people who weigh more than they should, do not get enough exercise, or have bad posture are at risk.

Noticeable symptoms: Numbness or tingling in the hands, especially at night, is a major symptom. The numbness or tingling is in all but the little finger because that finger receives signals from a different nerve, one that does not pass through the carpal tunnel. Hands may also become "clumsy" as a loss of strength develops, making it more difficult to grasp and hold objects between the thumb and fingers. Some people feel pain in their hands, wrists, and sometimes arms or shoulders.

Diagnosis: A healthcare worker will ask you to bend back your hand to test the flexibility of the wrist. You may squeeze a device that measures strength of the hands and fingers. Another test involves holding the hands together as if praying, but upside down; after a few moments the healthcare worker will ask about numbness or tingling. He or she will also tap the hands and arms lightly and ask about tingling sensations; the diagnostician may also ask which fingers are affected by tingling and numbness. These tests will determine whether the problem is caused by carpal tunnel syndrome and will also show the seriousness of any damage.

In some cases the healthcare worker may do a nerve conduction study, or electromyography (ih-LEHK-troh-miy-AHG-ruh-fee). For this test he or she inserts needles at several places on the arm, then runs very low voltage electricity through the needles. The test shows the location of any nerve damage.

Treatment options: Treatment for carpal tunnel syndrome begins with rest. The patient must temporarily give up activities that strain the hands and wrists. Moist heat and cold packs often help to ease the pain. The healthcare worker may prescribe oral anti-inflammatory drugs such as ibuprofen, naproxen, or aspirin for pain relief and to reduce inflammation. If there is a lot of pain and if oral anti-inflammatory drugs do not help, the healthcare worker may inject cortisone. However, cortisone can cause unwanted side effects.

A doctor may recommend wearing a wrist splint on the injured wrist while sleeping to keep the hand and wrist level. Sometimes the splint is also worn during the day to relieve pressure on the nerve. If these measures do not work, surgery may be necessary to relieve pressure on the nerve. However, only a small percentage of people with carpal tunnel syndrome require surgery.

The healthcare worker will also probably send the patient to a licensed physical therapist, who will help rebuild weakened muscles and teach stretching exercises designed to make arms and wrists more flexible.

Stages and progress: The longer carpal tunnel syndrome goes untreated, the more extensive the nerve damage will be. The muscles of the shoulders, arms, and hands become weak, and other repetitive strain injuries may develop.

Prevention and risk factors: Carpal tunnel syndrome is usually caused by rapidly repeated motions. When the wrist is held in an awkward position or force is used during such activities, the likelihood of injury increases.

Four things can be done to reduce the chances of getting carpal tunnel syndrome: (1) Learn how to do repetitive tasks in ways that will not strain the hands, wrists, and arms. (2) Take frequent breaks when doing repetitive tasks. (3) Use only as much force as is absolutely necessary to get a job done. (4) Do stretching exercises to keep muscles flexible before beginning and after finishing a task. If you spend more than about an hour at a task, take a break and do stretching exercises.

Effects on American population and health: The National Institutes of Health estimates that 2 million Americans have stress conditions including carpal tunnel syndrome. In 1998, 392,000 cases of workplace illnesses were reported to the Bureau of Labor Statistics. Of these 65% (253,300) were repetitive. In 1999, 246,700 cases of repetitive stress were reported.

Repetitive stress injuries can be caused by keyboarding or other tasks that use the same motions over and over. Stopping the repetitive motions from time to time—say every hour or so—and stretching the muscles involved helps prevent this kind of injury. For keyboarding, a good stretching break includes making a fist and then spreading the fingers, which should be repeated several times, relaxing the hands before going back to the keyboard. Similar stretching exercises should be used before starting keyboarding.

Cartilage

BODY SYSTEM

Cartilage is a flexible substance that precedes bone development in children and that is found in adults at *joints*, places where bones meet, as well as in organs that combine stiffness with flexibility.

Although cartilage is found in all vertebrates, such as bony fish, amphibians, reptiles, birds, and mammals, it is especially prominent in sharks and rays, which have skeletons of cartilage instead of bone.

Size, role, and location: Most cartilage in an adult covers joints. It also forms a strengthening framework in the nose and exterior ears; in flexible tubes such as the bronchi, esophagus, and trachea; and in the larynx. Considerable cartilage occurs as part of the spinal column and attached to the ribs.

There are three main types of cartilage: white, yellow, and fibrous. All three consist of cells and cell products such as fibers made from a substance called *collagen* (KOL-uh-juhn), but cartilage does not contain blood vessels or nerves. Some people refer only to the fibers and the matrix the fibers are in as cartilage. A membrane around each structure made from cartilage contains blood vessels as well as stem cells that migrate into the cartilage to become cartilage-producing cells.

Conditions that affect cartilage: Joint diseases, such as rheumatoid arthritis or osteoarthritis, are diseases of cartilage more than of bone or ligament, although other tissues are involved. Many autoimmune diseases attack connective tissue, especially collagen, and therefore are diseases of cartilage.

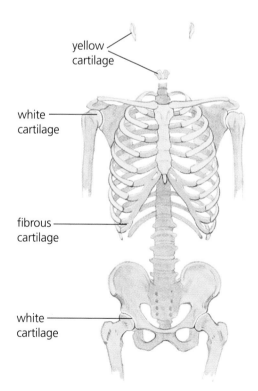

yellow cartilage

white cartilage

fibrous cartilage

white cartilage

Three kinds of cartilage
Yellow cartilage is in the larynx and ears. Fibrous cartilage is in the spinal column and attached to ribs. White cartilage is found at certain movable joints.

Conditions that affect the structure of the nose are basically disorders of cartilage. Some genetic disorders that affect cartilage result in extreme height or in short stature.

Cartilage that is damaged is slow to heal. It can sometimes break, with a piece lodging in a part of the joint where it does not belong. In that case the fragment needs to be surgically removed.

The cartilage that attaches the ribs to the *sternum* can become painfully inflamed. The exact cause of this condition is not known, but it usually returns to normal after a short time. A rare cancer can occur in cartilage, but it is slow growing and usually can be successfully removed with surgery.

Cataract
(KAAT-uh-raakt)

DISEASE

TYPE: MECHANICAL

See also
Allergies
Down syndrome
Eyes and vision
Rubella ("German" measles)
Viruses and disease

In young people the lens of the eye is normally transparent. For a variety of reasons this transparency may decrease over time. The lens takes on a degree of clouding, or opacity, that causes increasingly blurry vision. This condition is known as a cataract.

Cause: There are many different causes of cataracts. The so-called *senile cataract,* by far the most common, is caused by long-term exposure to the ultraviolet portion of sunlight. Over time the higher energy light waves "cook" protein fibers in the lens. Just as boiling causes the liquid albumin of an egg to turn to solid white, so light causes the fibers to exude a yellow-brown pigment that clouds vision. This rarely occurs in persons less than 50 years of age.

Less frequent causes of cataracts are poor nutrition, a history of allergic skin reactions, direct injury to the eye, severe diabetes, smoking, contact with certain poisons, and the taking of some steroid drugs.

A condition known as *congenital* (present at birth) *cataract* occurs rarely in infants. Congenital cataracts may occur as the result of a pregnant woman's becoming infected with a viral disease, especially rubella (German measles). Congenital cataracts may also occur as a side effect of certain genetic conditions such as Down syndrome.

Incidence: Almost everyone over 65 has some degree of senile cataract in one or both eyes, though people who spend a great deal of time in sunlight may experience problems sooner.

Medicare records show that 30 million American senior citizens have surgery to correct cataracts. Around the world cataract is the leading cause of blindness, accounting for 42% despite the existence of a sure cure with surgery.

Studies released in 2000 show that men who are obese have a higher cataract risk, especially taller men.

Noticeable symptoms: All cataracts are painless. Except in the case of congenital cataract, the condition usually becomes apparent only with age. The first signs may come in the form of reduced sensitivity to different colors and in problems with glare, particularly associated with night driving. Farsighted people may be pleasantly surprised to find that they can read without glasses, a temporary phenomenon sometimes called "second sight." Eventually, however, some degree of blurring usually occurs, or perhaps double vision or other distortions.

Diagnosis: Using a handheld ophthalmoscope (of-THAAL-muh-SKOHP) (lighted device for observing the interior of the eye), a physician can track the size, location, and severity of a cataract almost from the beginning. As the condition progresses, clouding may become observable even without instruments, appearing as a dull whitish area in the center of the eye. It was once common practice to delay surgical treatment until the cataract "ripened" to the point that vision was greatly impaired. But today, with cataract surgery an outstanding success in 95% of cases, the usual practice is to operate whenever the patient begins to experience a degree of loss that interferes with normal activities.

Treatment options: Short of surgical removal of the clouded lens, there is no effective way to reverse the vision changes related to cataracts. But stronger prescription glasses or contact lenses, as well as improved lighting in work areas, can often postpone treatment.

Eventually, however, the only reasonable course of treatment for otherwise healthy individuals is surgical removal of the clouded lens and replacement of the lens with another means of focusing—usually a plastic lens sewn into the eye called an *intraocular* (IHN-truh-OK-yuh-luhr) *implant*. The replacement lens is permanently implanted in the space previously occupied by the natural lens. Such cataract surgery is the most frequently performed of all operations in persons over 65.

The operation itself typically takes about an hour and is performed in a hospital or ophthalmic clinic on an outpatient basis. In the most frequently used procedure the patient is given local or general anesthesia, after which the surgeon makes a small half-moon incision around the upper edge of the cornea, using a fine diamond-tipped instrument. After a small amount of clear gel is injected into the space surrounding the clouded lens, the lens itself is removed as a solid mass or, more commonly, emulsified by sound waves and vacuumed away.

Finally, the artificial implant is slipped in place and the incision closed with a stitch or two. Upon waking, the patient is given antibiotics and sent home. Full recovery is almost immediate, though patients may be instructed to wear a patch for a few hours and to avoid stooping, strenuous activity, or physical strain for several days. The body absorbs the thread, and the incision typically heals completely in a month.

In a minority of patients for whom intraocular implants are not recommended, prescription glasses or contact lenses are alternatives.

Stay out of sun

Don't smoke

Prevention and risk factors: Exposure to sunlight is the main risk factor, but diabetes doubles the risk and also lowers the age at which cataracts occur. To reduce the effect of bright sunlight on the eye, wear ultraviolet-screening sunglasses or ultraviolet-screening coatings on prescription glasses commonly worn outdoors. Such protection is especially necessary at higher altitudes, since layers of atmosphere reduce the amount of ultraviolet radiation. People with diabetes can slow the progress of cataracts by proper monitoring and control of their blood sugar. And, of course, stop smoking.

History: Cataracts get their name from the ancient Greeks, who believed that the whiteness seen behind the pupil of the eye was a kind of waterfall descending from the brain. Cataract surgery of a primitive sort is thought be 3,000 years old. Surgeons known as "couchers" simply punched the clouded lens of their blind patients into the interior of the eye. While this provided temporary improvement in sight, the long-term results were the almost total loss of vision. The first successful attempt at cataract surgery as practiced today was in France in 1756. The first artificial plastic implants were introduced in the 1950s.

Cat-scratch fever

DISEASE

TYPE: INFECTIOUS
(BACTERIAL)

See also
Animal diseases and humans
Bacteria and disease
Pets and disease

Many people, particularly children, who are scratched by healthy cats develop cat-scratch fever, which is characterized by a minor inflammation in the scratched area, followed by swelling of the lymph nodes and fever.

Cause: Cat-scratch fever is caused almost exclusively by a small rod-shaped bacterium, *Bartonella henselae*. Almost all cases follow contact with cats and typically involve cat scratches or bites—rarely dog scratches or bites. Cat fleas also may spread the disease when they bite humans.

Incidence: Cat-scratch fever is a common disease all over the world, though rare in the United States. Most cases occur in children under the age of 17, with the majority in children under the age of 12. AIDS patients and other people with compromised immune systems are most at risk for becoming seriously ill from cat-scratch fever.

Noticeable symptoms: Within three to ten days after being infected, a small, pus-filled lesion develops at the site of the scratch or other wound. As nearby lymph nodes become infected—within two weeks—they become enlarged and tender. This stage is accompanied by fever, headache, fatigue, and lack of appetite. The symptoms usually persist for two to four months, after which most people recover completely.

Diagnosis: A doctor will suspect cat-scratch fever if a patient has recently been scratched by a cat and has inflamed lymph nodes. The doctor may perform a skin test; if the skin reacts positively to a substance called cat-scratch antigen, the diagnosis is confirmed. Sometimes diagnosis includes a biopsy of an affected lymph node—taking a sample of cells from the node—to look for bacteria.

Treatment options: In many cases no treatment is necessary: The disease runs its course and disappears spontaneously. Sometimes a doctor may prescribe an antibiotic, such as tetracycline, to speed the course of recovery.

Cerebral palsy

(SEHR-uh-bruhl PAWL-zee)

DISORDER

TYPE: DEVELOPMENTAL

See also
Brain
Childbirth, complications of
Developmental disability
Epilepsy
Head injuries
Jaundice
Meningitis
Muscles
Rubella ("German" measles)

Cerebral palsy is a group of disorders that result from damage to particular areas of the brain—the areas that control movement. The parts of the body most impaired are those that must move freely to function, such as the arms and legs and the tongue and other organs involved in speech.

The damage responsible for cerebral palsy occurs only while the brain is still immature—either during development before birth, during birth itself, or during early childhood.

Types: There are several forms of the disease.

Spastic: This is by far the most common form and also the one that varies most widely in severity. The muscles, particularly in the arms and legs, are abnormally contracted, or stiff, and subject to tremors. The parts of the body affected can be grouped as *hemiplegia* (HEHM-ih-PLEE-jee-uh), with the arm and leg on only one side affected; *diplegia* (diy-PLEE-jee-uh), affecting only the legs; or *quadriplegia* (KWOD-ruh-PLEE-jee-uh), with both arms and legs affected, along with the trunk and mouth.

The most typical symptom is difficulty in walking. Persistently contracted thigh muscles may cause the knees and feet to turn, or *scissor,* inward. Stiff calf muscles may cause *toe walking.* Mildly affected children may display only slight clumsiness in their movements. Others, however, are unable to manage even the simplest voluntary motions.

Severe spasticity may prevent the muscles from stretching and lengthening as the bones grow. The muscles may become permanently shortened and stiffened, to become *contractures.*

Athetoid (AATH-uh-toid), or *dyskinetic:* Typical symptoms are spontaneous, involuntary movements, such as jerks or writhing. Those affected have trouble keeping their bodies stable, whether standing or sitting. The involuntary movements also make walking and speech difficult.

Ataxic: This form weakens the sense of balance, the perception of depth and distance, and the ability to reach objects accurately or to identify them by touch. Walking is unsteady, and activities that require precise coordination, such as writing, may be impaired.

Mixed: Some of those affected have symptoms of more than one form of the disease. Such mixed cerebral palsy

Although a child may have many of the problems associated with cerebral palsy, many learn as they grow to cope with their disabilities and are able to attend school, hold jobs, and lead lives that are normal in most ways.

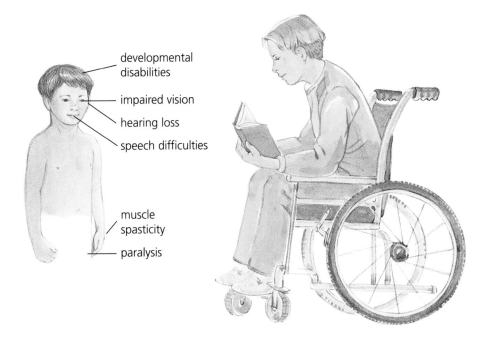

developmental disabilities

impaired vision

hearing loss

speech difficulties

muscle spasticity

paralysis

reflects damage in more than one area of the brain and is likely to be especially severe.

Other problems are associated with cerebral palsy as well, including loss of hearing, impaired vision, and difficulties with eating and speech. Many affected children have at least occasional problems with bowel control. Furthermore, cerebral palsy is often accompanied by other central nervous system disorders, such as developmental disability (mental retardation) and epilepsy.

Cause: In many instances the precise cause of the brain damage cannot be determined. There are several conditions, however, that are known to cause brain damage, or at least to raise the risk of its occurrence.

It was once thought that most cerebral palsy is caused by asphyxia during birth, in which a baby is deprived of sufficient oxygen during a difficult or prolonged delivery. But evidence now suggests that most damage occurs during prenatal development, well before birth.

The risk of a child having cerebral palsy can be raised by a number of harmful factors during pregnancy, including maternal infections such as rubella ("German" measles) and conditions such as Rh incompatibility that cause jaundice in newborns. Premature birth, for whatever reason, also raises the risk of brain damage and subsequent cerebral palsy.

In early childhood brain damage may result from a severe infection such as meningitis or from a violent head injury.

Incidence: Though less prevalent than developmental disability, cerebral palsy is among the more common defects of the nervous system. It is diagnosed in two to three per thousand children three years old or more. About 500,000 Americans of all ages are affected.

About 70% of persons with cerebral palsy have the spastic type, about 20% the athetoid type, and about 10% the ataxic.

Noticeable symptoms: Early signs are difficult to identify, especially if the disorder is mild. An affected child may be unusually slow in learning to walk or talk—but this occurs in many normal children as well. By age two or three, however, the characteristic impairments of movement and speech are usually unmistakable.

Diagnosis: Neurological tests and such imaging techniques as an MRI scan may reveal early signs of the brain damage responsible for cerebral palsy, but reliable diagnosis may not be possible before the age of two to three.

Treatment options: Cerebral palsy cannot be cured, but some of its harmful effects can be minimized. Team effort, including drug therapy, physical therapy, occupational therapy, speech therapy, orthopedic treatment, special education, and (in some cases) surgery, is often required. The goals are to minimize disability, to avoid secondary complications such as contractures, and to enable the affected person to live as normally as possible.

Outlook: For some cerebral palsy is a mild condition that does not interfere much with ordinary life. For most, however, it causes serious, lifelong disability. Severely affected individuals may be unable to lead fully independent lives, not only because of their physical limitations, but also because of developmental disability.

Cervical and uterine cancers

Abnormal bleeding or discharge from a woman's vagina may indicate the presence of a cervical or uterine cancer. When caught early, before they have spread to other organs, these cancers can usually be cured with treatment.

Parts affected: The uterus is the organ in a woman's body where an embryo grows into a baby. The embryo attaches to the lining of the uterus, called the *endometrium* (EHN-doh-MEE-tree-uhm). At the time of birth the baby leaves its mother's body through the lower part of the uterus. This narrow opening of the uterus, which leads to the vagina, is the *cervix* (SUHR-vihks).

Cause: Various factors appear to increase a woman's susceptibility to cervical/uterine cancers.

Most cervical cancer is linked to sexually transmitted diseases (STDs). Certain human papillomaviruses that cause genital warts appear to be the major cause. Other STDs associated with cervical cancer include herpes and chlamydia. Women who began having sexual intercourse at an early age, have had many sexual partners, or have a history of STDs are at increased risk of developing cervical cancer. Cigarette smoking also is associated with cervical cancer.

Uterine cancer typically arises in the endometrium and is also called *endometrial cancer*. Susceptibility is linked to the endometrium's exposure to estrogen, a hormone that stimulates cell division. The greater the cumulative exposure to estrogen, the greater the risk of uterine cancer. Thus uterine cancer usually occurs in older women either during or following menopause. Women who began menstruating early, began menopause late, or never had children are at higher risk. So too are women who take estrogen replacement therapy that consists only of estrogen (as opposed to estrogen plus progesterone). The drug tamoxifen, used to treat breast cancer, increases the risk slightly. Obesity, diabetes, and hypertension also are risk factors.

Incidence: Each year approximately 13,000 American women are diagnosed with invasive cervical cancer and 38,000 with uterine cancer. Incidence rates for cervical cancer are higher among black women than white women; the reverse is true for uterine cancer. About 11,000 deaths from cervical and uterine cancers occur annually.

Noticeable symptoms: Cervical and uterine cancers develop long before they produce detectable symptoms. The first symptom a woman is likely to notice is abnormal vaginal bleeding or watery discharge. If a cancer has spread to nearby tissues, it is said to be invasive. Symptoms of invasive cervical and uterine cancers may include fatigue, weight loss, backaches, leg pain, and difficult urination. ***A woman who experiences any of these symptoms should see a doctor as soon as possible.***

Phone doctor

Diagnosis: The doctor will conduct a complete pelvic examination. A *Pap smear*, which scrapes tissue from the cervix, will be performed and checked for abnormal cells. The Pap smear can detect cells that will become cervical cancer even before cancer has started. Ultrasound may be used to look for causes of the woman's symptoms. If suspicious cells are detected, a *biopsy* will be performed. In this procedure a small amount of tissue is removed from the suspect area and examined under a microscope. A procedure called *dilation and curettage* (D&C) may be performed to obtain endometrial tissue for examination. If the biopsy or D&C confirms cancer, blood studies and other tests can help determine the stage of the disease.

Stages and progress: Knowing the stage of a cancer enables a physician to choose the most effective treatment. Staging describes the size of the tumor and whether it has spread to other organs. A widely used system assigns a stage of I, II, III, or IV. I is an early stage, with no indication that the cancer has spread beyond the cervix or uterus. IV is the most advanced stage, with the cancer having spread, or *metastasized*, to distant parts of the body. The more advanced the cancer, the more difficult it is to treat.

Treatment options: Early noninvasive cervical cancer may be removed surgically, using a scalpel or laser. Alternate treatments include destroying the cancerous cells by freezing them (cyrotherapy) or exposing them to intense heat (electrocoagulation). Invasive cervical cancer is treated by surgery, radiation, and perhaps chemotherapy.

Early uterine cancer is usually treated by surgery. Especially in patients who have children or with later stages of cervical or uterine cancer, complete removal of the uterus and cervix may be performed (a *hysterectomy*). Removal of all the female sex organs including the ovaries is called a *total hysterectomy*. If the cancer has spread beyond the uterus, radiation therapy typically follows surgery. Chemotherapy may also be used.

During the five years following treatment, patients are advised to have regular, frequent medical checkups to watch for recurrence of the cancer. Assuming no recurrence, annual checkups are recommended after the first five years.

Prevention and possible actions: Early detection greatly improves women's chances of being successfully cured of cervical and uterine cancers. A woman should have a Pap smear and pelvic exam every year after age 18 or after becoming sexually active. Pap smears can detect abnormal cervical cells before they become cancerous. Safe-sex practices lower the risk of sexually transmitted diseases that may lead to cervical cancer. A well-balanced diet, regular exercise, and avoidance of tobacco products lower the risk of cervical/uterine cancers.

Chest pain

SYMPTOM

See also
Angina
Bronchitis
Cancers
Embolism
Fractures, dislocations, sprains, and strains
Fungus diseases
GERD (gastroesophageal reflux disease)
Heart attack
Heartburn
Pleurisy
Pneumonia
Scleroderma
Shingles

Chest pain can range from a dull pressure or ache to a burning sensation or a severe squeezing or crushing feeling. Although people often connect chest pain to heart attack, there are a number of different injuries, disorders, and diseases that can also cause chest pain.

Parts affected: Chest pain may occur anywhere from the neck down to the bottom of the ribs. Most of the organs located in the chest can produce pain, but commonly pain originates in a muscle or in the esophagus, heart, or lungs. Inflammation of the lining of the chest, or pleurisy, is a cause of chest pain.

Related symptoms: Severe crushing pain that starts over the heart and moves up to the neck and shoulders may mean that the heart is not getting enough oxygen—a heart attack. A recurring pain in the chest may be angina, which is also caused by heart disease.

Pain caused by a heart problem is often accompanied by sweating, nausea, dizziness, or difficulty in breathing. Pale, blue, cold, or clammy skin is another sign. If the heart is deprived of sufficient oxygen for too long, a heart attack can induce loss of consciousness or be fatal.

Coughing, shortness of breath, or an above normal temperature may accompany bronchitis, pneumonia, or other causes of chest pain. Pleurisy tends to produce severe pain on one side of the chest only. A sharp pain that appears from nowhere may be a lung clot (*pulmonary embolism*). **Contact an emergency medical service immediately since this condition may be fatal if not treated.** Another equally dangerous lung condition, spontaneously collapsed lung, is marked by milder chest pain that increases while inhaling.

Call ambulance

Heartburn is typically accompanied by an acid taste in the mouth. The pain may increase in postures that push up the stomach or lower the esophagus.

A pain that appears only when moving the upper body, arms, or neck is usually caused by a pulled muscle.

Associations: Bronchitis or pneumonia may cause pain deep in the chest. Several diseases produced when a fungus invades the lungs also produce chest pain.

The burning in the chest due to heartburn is the result of stomach acid backing up into the esophagus, a condition more formally known as GERD (gastroesophageal reflux disease). The esophagus may also cause pain through spasms or incomplete emptying of food, called *achalasia* (AAK-uh-LAY-zhuh). Diseases such as scleroderma or cancer can also produce esophageal pain.

A burning feeling in the skin on one side of the chest may be due to a viral infection called shingles.

Prevention and possible actions: Stretching and other warm-ups can help prevent muscle pulls. A diet low in fat and cholesterol helps reduce heart problems. Small meals are less likely to cause heartburn.

Phone doctor

Pain with symptoms of heart attack, lung clot, or collapsed lung should receive immediate medical attention. ***It is best not to ignore any type of chest pain. Consult a physician as to the cause.***

Relief of symptoms: Pain from bronchitis or pneumonia can be relieved with rest, use of a humidifier, and cough medicine. An antacid normally relieves heartburn, which is one way of distinguishing heartburn from heart attack, which is not relieved by antacids. Application of an ice pack will often ease the pain of a pulled muscle. Heart attack or severe lung problems must be treated by a physician.

Chicken pox

DISEASE

TYPE: INFECTIOUS (VIRAL)

See also
Blister
Itching
Rashes
Reye's syndrome
Shingles
Viruses and disease

Nearly everyone has had experience with chicken pox, although often so early in life that the unpleasant, itchy time in bed has been forgotten. But thanks to the introduction of an effective vaccine, chicken pox, also known as *varicella* (VEHR-ih-SEHL-uh), is becoming as rare as measles or mumps.

Cause: *Varicella zoster* is the virus that causes chicken pox. It is carried in saliva and mucus and can be spread when an infected person coughs or sneezes. After a person is infected with *Varicella*, the virus produces the symptoms known as chicken pox. Then it hides. The virus remains hidden in the body in nerves or in the brain. It remains dormant there for years. Later in life it may become active and cause shingles, a condition with pain in the infected nerve and a rash on the body or face.

Varicella zoster is in the herpes family of viruses. All the herpes viruses are able to hide from the immune system. They emerge and attack when the immune system has been weakened, often by stress.

Incidence: Chicken pox is one of the most common viral infections of children. Almost 90% of those exposed become infected. In 1998 in the United States 120,000 cases were reported. The largest number of cases occurs in winter and early spring. Most children become infected between the ages of six and ten.

Noticeable symptoms: The most obvious symptom is a rash that starts on the body and scalp and spreads to the face, arms, and legs. A fever may also be present. The person with chicken pox may feel tired and generally ill.

Diagnosis: A doctor will want to examine the rash. Since rashes can have many different causes, it is best to have a doctor diagnose the disease in person instead of over the telephone. He or she may ask about contact with other children who have chicken pox or measles or other diseases that cause rashes. A blood sample will reveal a low white blood cell count.

Treatment options: Since chicken pox is caused by a virus, antibiotics or other medicines cannot knock it out. One has to depend on the immune system. Antiviral medications, such as acyclovir, can help reduce the severity of chicken pox, especially in individuals with faulty immune systems.

A physician can prescribe lotions or creams to reduce the itchiness of the rash and to help dry it up. Antihistamines may also relieve some of the itchiness. Showers with a mild soap help prevent the sores from becoming infected with bacteria.

Avoid aspirin

Pain-relieving medicine may be prescribed if blisters form in the mouth or close to the eyes. *Aspirin should never be taken to relieve chicken pox symptoms.* Sometimes when people with chicken pox take aspirin, they develop a condition called Reye's syndrome, which can be fatal. *Call the physician if symptoms such as excessive sleepiness or difficult breathing develop; these could signal Reye's syndrome.*

Phone doctor

If a pregnant woman, premature baby, person with a compromised immune system or other susceptible condition is exposed to chicken pox, he or she may be advised to take *Varicella zoster* immune globulin (VZIG) to reduce the risk of illness.

Stages and progress: The virus usually gets in the body through the mouth or nose. It incubates for one to three weeks before the characteristic rash develops on the body. For a day or so before the rash the infected person begins to feel ill, with a slight fever, fatigue, and loss of appetite.

At first the rash consists of tiny red spots. These grow somewhat and become filled with fluid; at this stage the rash becomes small blisters. These blisters can be very itchy. Over several days the rash or blisters spread to the face and limbs. The fluid-filled blisters dry out and form scabs. It is important to keep from scratching these scabs to prevent long-lasting scars.

Separate rash outbreaks occur over several days. Each starts on the body and spreads out to the face and limbs. The infected person will have new rash blisters and dried scabs at the same time. After a week to ten days the disease runs its course in children, and they feel well again. Rarely, chicken pox leads to pneumonia or brain damage. Fewer than 100 children in the United States die from the disease each year.

Adults infected with *Varicella* may have more noticeable flulike symptoms before breaking out in a rash. Often it takes longer for an adult to recover from chicken pox than a child. An adult is also more likely to develop complications, such as pneumonia or encephalitis. Another group that may experience severe symptoms are babies who contract the disease from their mothers while in the womb.

Prevention: Chicken pox is spread person to person by saliva and mucus droplets in the air. A person infected with the *Varicella* virus can pass it to others before he or she shows symptoms. Chicken pox can also be spread by contact with the fluid in the blisters of the rash. The blisters remain infective until all traces of the fluid are gone. Good personal health habits—covering the mouth and nose when coughing or sneezing—help prevent transmission. Still, in the past almost 90% of all children got chicken pox.

Recently, a new option became available. There is now a vaccine to protect people from chicken pox. The vaccine is 70 to 90% effective; vaccinated individuals who do get chicken pox have a mild illness that runs its course quickly. Young children should have a single dose of the vaccine when they are getting their other immunizations. Older children—to the age of 12—who have not had chicken pox should also be vaccinated with a single dose. Any adult who has not had chicken pox should get two doses of chicken pox vaccine, four to eight weeks apart. More than 70% of those vaccinated are protected from chicken pox. By 2001 vaccination for chicken pox was a requirement for entry into school in most of the United States.

Most children and adults can take the chicken pox vaccine safely. Exceptions are pregnant women and anyone with cancer or an illness that harms the immune system.

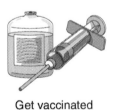
Get vaccinated

Childbirth, complications of

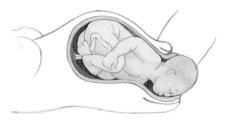

Normal childbirth
As a fetus approaches birth, it should move into position with its head down. Just before birth, the fetus turns and faces the mother's back, but if there is premature rupture of the membranes, the birth process begins before the fetus has reached the correct position.

Childbirth used to be a very dangerous process, resulting in the deaths of many mothers and babies. Thanks to modern medicine it is now remarkably safe. The rate of death for newborn babies is quite low, and for mothers, even lower. Nevertheless, certain conditions known as complications may occur before, during, or immediately after birth. These may require special medical attention to prevent death or lasting harm. Among the more serious complications are the following.

Preterm birth: One of the greatest dangers a baby can encounter is birth before full term—that is, before the body systems are mature enough to ensure survival. The lungs of a baby born too early may not be able to breathe air, the body itself may not generate enough heat for warmth, and the digestive system may not be able to transform food into nourishment.

Bed rest, certain drugs, and other measures may help prevent or slow premature labor. If premature delivery is considered imminent, corticosteroid drugs given to the mother may help speed up development of the baby's lungs. When preterm birth does occur, facilities dedicated to intensive care for infants can help keep babies alive until their systems develop.

Premature rupture of membranes (PROM): Normally, when pregnancy reaches full term, the "bag of waters," the balloonlike sac of membranes around the baby in the uterus, breaks and releases amniotic fluid either just before or just after labor begins. Sometimes, however, the membranes break open prematurely.

There are two types of premature rupture of membranes. In the more common type the baby is mature, but the break and resulting flow of amniotic fluid occur an hour or more before labor begins. Without the protection of the membrane sac the baby runs an increased risk of infection. Without the cushion of amniotic fluid the umbilical cord is more likely to be compressed (see below). The standard treatment is to hasten delivery by chemically induced labor or by surgical delivery (*cesarean section*).

The second type is called preterm premature rupture of membranes. It occurs before the fetus is fully developed and is likely to trigger preterm birth. A balanced medical strategy must be employed. On the one hand, medications and other methods are used to delay delivery until development is more complete; on the other, if infection or other threats become serious, immediate delivery may be necessary even if the baby is premature.

Abnormal presentation: Most babies, by the time they are ready to be born, are positioned head down in the uterus facing the mother's back. This is the safest and easiest presentation for birth. Other positions, with the head up and the legs or buttocks down (called *breech presentation*), cause difficulties with delivery and may require cesarean section.

Cephalopelvic (sehf-uh-loh-PEHL-vihk) **disproportion:** The largest single part of a baby is its head. Sometimes the head (*cephalos* in Greek) is too big to pass through the ring of the mother's *pelvic bones*. If the disproportion is severe enough, a cesarean delivery may be necessary.

Umbilical cord compression: Until a baby is born and breathing air, the hollow umbilical cord between the placenta and the baby's navel is a vital lifeline for the delivery of oxygen. Without a steady supply of oxygen the baby will suffer dangerous *hypoxia* (see below).

Before or during labor the cord may become compressed—squeezed so that blood circulation through it is reduced or cut off. The cord may be tightly wrapped around the baby's body, or it may slip forward (*prolapse*) into the birth canal and get trapped between the baby and the canal wall. The cord can sometimes be freed during ordinary delivery, but an emergency cesarean may be necessary.

Asphyxia and hypoxia: Before birth all the oxygen that a baby needs must be supplied by the mother, carried in blood and transferred through the placenta and umbilical cord. At birth this source is cut off, and oxygen must be absorbed from the baby's own lungs.

If the oxygen supply is interrupted, the baby quickly suffers oxygen deprivation, or asphyxia. The resulting lack of oxygen in the body tissues, known as hypoxia, may cause death or permanent damage. For example, hypoxia is thought to trigger bleeding into the brain, which in turn is believed to be a major cause of cerebral palsy, epilepsy, and hydrocephalus.

Before birth asphyxia may result from several conditions, ranging from preeclampsia to prolonged labor. The main solution is to deliver the baby as soon as possible, by cesarean section if necessary.

If a newborn baby does not breathe properly, *resuscitation* measures are used to prevent asphyxia (see Respiratory distress below).

Respiratory distress: For any of several reasons a newborn baby may have trouble breathing properly, a condition known as respiratory distress. The baby might have *wet lung syndrome,* for example: The lungs fail to become entirely free of the fluid that filled them before birth and cannot absorb enough oxygen. Or the airways may be clogged or irritated by *meconium* (mih-KOH-nee-um), waste material released from the baby's bowel into the amniotic fluid. Or the normal flow of nervous impulses that control breathing may be impaired, causing temporary *apnea* (AAP-nee-uh), or "non-breathing."

A variety of resuscitation measures are used to stimulate breathing and to ensure a supply of oxygen to the lungs. They range from simply massaging the chest and suctioning out meconium to providing oxygen mechanically.

Persistent pulmonary hypertension: Before a baby's birth the lungs are inactive, and only a small amount of blood is required to fulfill their needs. The *pulmonary blood vessels* serving the lungs are constricted, raising the pressure but lowering the volume of blood passing through them. This pattern of high blood pressure and low blood flow in the lungs combined with low blood pressure and high blood flow through the rest of the body is known as *fetal circulation.*

At birth a major shift in circulation normally occurs. The lungs expand and fill with air. The pulmonary blood vessels relax and *dilate* (open), lowering blood pressure in the lungs and increasing blood flow, circulating enough blood to absorb oxygen from the lungs. But occasionally, for a variety of reasons, the shift fails to take place when it should. The pulmonary vessels remain constricted (narrow), so lung blood pressure remains high and blood flow low. Without sufficient blood to absorb oxygen from the lungs the baby may suffer asphyxia and hypoxia (see above). This condition is known as persistent pulmonary hypertension, or *persistent fetal circulation.*

Treatment has two aims. The first is to increase flow through the pulmonary blood vessels. Drugs and other techniques are used to dilate blood vessels and stimulate the heart. The other aim is to increase the oxygen supply to the lungs using the resuscitation techniques applied to asphyxia generally.

Group B streptococcus infection: The human body is normally colonized by many kinds of bacteria, most of which are harmless. Among them are Group B streptococcus bacteria, which periodically colonize the lower intestine in men and women or the vagina in women. Group B streptococci tend to cause disease only among those with weak immune systems. Unfortunately, this group includes newborns, whose immune systems are not completely developed. Up to a third of women may be carriers of Group B strep when they go into labor, and a significant percentage of their babies may become infected during delivery.

Group B streptococcus infection is potentially very dangerous to newborns. It can cause sepsis ("blood poisoning"), pneumonia, or meningitis, which may be fatal or result in lasting disabilities.

The infection can be effectively treated with antibiotics, but prevention is better for overall health and safety. Pregnant women can be tested for the bacteria during late pregnancy and early labor and then given antibiotics to reduce or eliminate the bacteria population. Such screening and treatment are becoming increasingly routine.

Postpartum bleeding: After delivery natural contractions of the mother's uterus usually squeeze shut the blood vessels that formerly supplied it, so that normal postpartum bleeding, called *lochia* (LOH-kee-uh), occurs but is gradually reduced. Massage and administration of a hormone that encourages contractions are often used to help the process along. But sometimes dangerously heavy bleeding does occur. Excessive bleeding is treated with drugs that encourage clotting and, in rare instances, with surgery to close the blood vessels.

Chlamydia

(klaa-MIHD-ee-uh)

DISEASE

TYPE: MECHANICAL

See also
Bacteria and disease
Ectopic pregnancy
PID (pelvic inflammatory disease)
Pregnancy and disease
Reproductive system
STD (sexually transmitted diseases)

It is the most common reported disease in the United States, yet more than three-quarters of the women and almost half of the men who have it have no symptoms. The disease is chlamydia.

Cause: Chlamydia is caused by a bacterium, *Chlamydia trachomatis*. Most cases of chlamydia infection are the result of sexual transmission. If a woman has chlamydia during pregnancy, it can be passed to her offspring and cause blindness or severe pneumonia.

Incidence and risk factors: It is estimated that there are between 3 and 4 million new infections each year in the United States, making it the most common sexually transmitted disease.

Chlamydia is most frequently seen in 15 to 24 year olds. Risk factors include having more than one sex partner or a sex partner who has had many partners, having sex without a condom, and having a history of sexually transmitted diseases. Sexually abused children are also at high risk for chlamydia infection.

Noticeable symptoms: Symptoms of chlamydia are different in men and women. About 85% of women have no symptoms. Those who do may experience an abnormal discharge from the vagina, abdominal pain, bleeding between menstrual periods, and painful urination. Only 40% of men have no symptoms. Symptoms in most men consist of a discharge from the penis, painful or burning urination, and tender or swollen testicles.

Diagnosis: The symptoms of chlamydia are similar to those of gonorrhea. The doctor will do tests to determine exactly which sexually transmitted disease the person has, since treatments for chlamydia and gonorrhea are different. Swabs from the opening to the penis or from the vagina and cervix can be taken to get fluid for testing. A recently developed urine test may also be used.

Course of the disease: When symptoms occur, they may begin one to two weeks after infection. Prompt treatment is important because serious medical problems can occur if chlamydia infection is not treated. In women the infection can move into the upper part of the reproductive system and spread to the fallopian tubes and ovaries. It can also lead to pelvic inflammatory disease (PID), which can cause blockages in the fallopian tubes. Blocked tubes can result in pregnancy outside the uterus (ectopic pregnancy) or infertility.

In men untreated chlamydia infection can spread to the sperm ducts and cause sterility. About 1% of men with untreated chlamydia infection develop *Reiter's syndrome*—an infection of the urethra—sores on the penis and in the mouth, *conjunctivitis,* and *arthritis.*

Treatment: Chlamydia can be easily and effectively treated with antibiotics. Some effective antibiotics require only one dose; others must be taken daily for a week. It is important that both partners be treated at the same time and that they take the full course of medication. People being treated for chlamydia should abstain from sex during treatment and be checked by a doctor before beginning to have sex again.

Prevention: Like all sexually transmitted diseases, the only sure prevention is abstinence. For people who are sexually active, using either male or female condoms regularly is the best protection. Vaginal spermicidal gels and creams can also help, but they are not as effective as condoms. There is also some evidence that spermicidal creams and gels that contain nonoxynol-9 can cause irritation that increases the risk of HIV infection. For this reason some doctors recommend the use only of creams and gels that do not contain nonoxynol-9. Condoms with nonoxynol-9 are still considered safe because the concentrations are much lower than in creams and gels.

People who are at high risk for chlamydia infection are encouraged to get regular screening (once or twice a year) for chlamydia as well as for other sexually transmitted diseases.

Global impact: Sexually transmitted diseases are a major problem throughout the world. The World Health Organization estimates that there are 89 million cases of chlamydia infection each year. Both industrialized and developing countries are affected, with people in their teens and twenties most likely to be infected.

Chloracne

(klawr-AAK-nee)

Chloracne, a chemically induced skin condition, is the only completely established effect on human beings of the chemicals known as dioxins. The best-known dioxin is a contaminant of a herbicide, but others occur in various chemicals that humans manufacture. These chemicals include some paints and varnishes and some oils used as lubricants in cutting tools.

Parts affected: Chloracne is a serious skin rash that appears on the face or on parts of the body that are exposed to dioxins or to many other chemical compounds based on chlorine. Ingestion or inhalation of dioxins also causes the symptom. The skin condition appears as blackheads and pimples on the face and neck or other parts of the body that have been exposed, often bare arms and hands. It may not respond to treatments for ordinary acne and may persist for many years after exposure to dioxin.

Related symptoms: Dioxins are considered among the most dangerous chemicals because even tiny amounts kill many different animals; effects on humans, other than inducing chloracne, have been hard to establish. Limited statistical evidence suggests that in humans dioxins may increase cancer rates, especially for soft-tissue cancers, lymphomas, multiple myeloma, or cancer of the liver or gallbladder.

Associations: There are about 75 dioxins that are produced at high temperatures in various chemical processes. Therefore they contaminate incinerator ashes as well as chlorine-based chemicals manufactured using high temperatures, such as bleaches used in making white paper. The most famous dioxin is 2,3,7,8-TCDD, a contaminant of insecticides and herbicides. It is the dioxin that contaminated the Agent Orange herbicide used by American soldiers to defoliate forests during the Vietnam War.

Prevention and possible actions: Chloracne occurs only in people who are exposed to chlorinated chemicals. Avoid contact with pesticides completely, and wash thoroughly soon after any contact with liquid paints, varnishes, or cutting oils.

Cholera

(KOL-ehr-uh)

DISEASE

TYPE: INFECTIOUS
(BACTERIAL)

See also
Bacteria and disease
Diarrhea
Epidemics

Phone doctor

Cholera is a serious intestinal disorder that causes severe diarrhea and vomiting. It is most common in less-developed countries that have poor sanitation facilities. People often get the disease as a result of drinking water contaminated with cholera bacteria. Foods such as shellfish and raw fruits and vegetables may also harbor the bacteria.

Cause: A comma-shaped bacterium called *Vibrio cholerae* causes cholera. Once vibrio bacteria are swallowed, they infect the mucous membrane of the small intestine. A toxin produced by the bacteria then makes bodily fluids flow quickly from the bloodstream into the intestines. Sudden, severe diarrhea and dehydration follow, leading to serious problems if left untreated.

Incidence: Cholera is rare in the United States. The few cases reported each year usually involve travelers returning from Asia or Africa, where the disease is far more widespread and has been known for centuries. Cholera also occurs in South and Central America, as well as in areas around the Mediterranean.

In 1992 the O139 variant of the cholera bacterium was discovered. It produces a more vigorous form of the disease. The O139 bacterium has infected people in India who had become immune to an earlier strain of cholera.

Noticeable symptoms: About one to five days after initial infection one may experience nausea, dizziness, and anxiousness. Next a watery, grayish-colored diarrhea begins. As much as a pint of water an hour may be lost as the diarrhea continues. Vomiting, without any feeling of nausea, often accompanies the diarrhea. If allowed to continue, the dehydration resulting from the diarrhea leads to intense thirst, muscle cramps, cold and withered skin, and more serious symptoms. *Seek medical help immediately.*

Diagnosis: Eliminating other causes of severe diarrhea and vomiting is an important part of diagnosing cholera. If you have recently returned from a country where cholera outbreaks are common, your doctor probably will suspect it. But a sample of your watery stool, which your doctor will send to a medical lab for testing, will probably be needed to confirm the presence of vibrio bacteria.

Treatment options: Replacing lost body fluids is an essential part of treating cholera and should begin soon after the diarrhea begins. Patients usually drink prescribed amounts of water containing sugar and certain other nutrients to restore the fluids that the diarrhea has drained out. If dehydration develops despite this treatment, the physician may decide to give fluids intravenously as well. Tetracycline hydrochloride or other antibiotics administered early on can help shorten the length of time one suffers with diarrhea.

Stages and progress: With proper treatment cholera normally runs its course quickly—from two to seven days—and patients usually recover completely. But if left untreated, the disease can cause serious problems because of the severe dehydration brought on by the diarrhea.

During the 1800s about half of all people who came down with cholera died. Today, when proper treatment is available, fewer than 10% of all cases prove fatal. The danger of death from cholera is usually greatest in underdeveloped nations, where medical facilities and supplies of clean water for treating dehydration are sometimes scarce. Cholera epidemics often make so many people sick at once that not enough healthy people remain to tend to them.

Prevention: Although cholera vaccines are available in some countries, they give only limited protection, and their use is not recommended by the U.S. Centers for Disease Control. As with many other waterborne infectious diseases, travelers must be careful about drinking contaminated water. As a general rule it is probably best to avoid local drinking water outside the United States and Canada. Only bottled drinks or drinking water that has been boiled can be considered safe in nations with poor sanitation. Watch out for ice in drinks as well. Cholera bacteria can also live for several days on fruits and vegetables, so these should not be eaten raw when the source is a location with endemic cholera.

Chromosomal abnormalities

DISORDER

TYPE: GENETIC

See also
Down syndrome
Fragile X syndrome
Genetic diseases

Within each regular cell of the body is a nucleus that directs the development and operations of that cell. The nucleus in human cells contains 46 *chromosomes* (KROH-muh-sohms). These chromosomes not only have the instruction set for cell operations, they also contain the genetic instructions—the *genes*—that determine the physical traits you inherit from your parents. Half the chromosomes come from each parent—23 from the father and 23 from the mother. The pairs are combined when the mother's egg is fertilized by the father's sperm.

Sometimes an abnormality occurs in either the formation or the combination of the chromosomes. The fertilized egg ends up with too many or too few chromosomes, or with chromosomes that are mixed or scrambled in some way.

Because each chromosome contains many genes, chromosomal abnormalities are likely to cause serious birth defects, affecting many body systems and often including developmental disability (mental retardation). Many of these defects are so severe that the offspring receiving them cannot survive. Of the abnormalities that do allow survival, the best known is Down

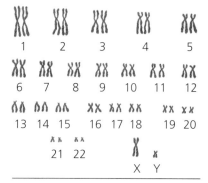

NORMAL CHROMOSOMES

1 2 3 4 5

6 7 8 9 10 11 12

13 14 15 16 17 18 19 20

21 22

X Y

ABNORMAL CHROMOSOMES

–extra portion
14

–extra portion
21

Chromosome pairs
The 23 pairs of chromosomes direct heredity and cell operations. When one chromosome combines with part of another or when there is an extra chromosome, development is seriously affected.

syndrome, which occurs when an extra copy of one specific chromosome is inherited, making a triplet instead of a pair.

There is one major exception to the rule that chromosomal abnormalities are noticeable at birth. Abnormalities in the number of the male (Y) or female (X) chromosomes that determine the offspring's sex tend to be far less severe. Sex-chromosome abnormalities include Klinefelter syndrome among boys (XXY or sometimes XXXY) and Turner syndrome among girls (one X, no Y).

Cause: No one knows exactly what causes chromosomal abnormalities to occur in particular fertilized eggs. Most occurrences appear to be accidental, caused by improper division of the cells that give rise to eggs or sperm.

Incidence: Scientists are just beginning to find out how common chromosomal abnormalities are. A large percentage of fetuses miscarry in early pregnancy, and it turns out that many of these have chromosomal abnormalities that prevent survival.

Noticeable symptoms: Chromosomal abnormalities (other than those that affect the sex chromosomes) are almost sure to be noticeable at birth.

Diagnosis: Microscopic examination of the chromosomes in a nucleus clearly shows such abnormalities. They can be identified before birth in fetal cells collected during a *prenatal test* such as amniocentesis (AAM-nee-oh-sehn-TEE-sihs).

Treatment options: Chromosomal abnormalities cannot be cured. Some symptoms, such as heart and digestive system malformations that are common in Down syndrome, can be remedied with surgery or other medical treatment.

Outlook: The outlook for affected children varies enormously. Some with sex-chromosome abnormalities lead entirely normal lives. At the other extreme are those so severely affected that they die before or shortly after birth. Even for a particular type of abnormality, such as Down syndrome, there is a wide range of abilities and physical conditions.

Risk factors: Chromosomal abnormalities are weakly familial: They occur more often in certain families, but not often enough to establish a clear pattern of inheritance. The main risk factor is the mother's age. Chromosomal abnormalities become increasingly common from the time a woman is 35 years old.

Chronic fatigue syndrome

DISEASE

TYPE: UNKNOWN CAUSE

This mysterious condition has been known by many names over the years, including *chronic mononucleosis* and *yuppie flu*. In England it is called *myalgic encephalitis,* while in Japan it is known as *natural killer cell syndrome.* In the United States chronic fatigue syndrome, or CFS, was first officially defined in 1987. Since then a great deal of research has been done to improve diagnosis (its symptoms have been redefined at least twice since 1987) and treatment.

Cause: Researchers have not yet determined the cause of CFS. The evidence suggests that CFS may be caused by a virus, a yeast infection, or a combination of causes. Other ideas suggested include anemia, low blood sugar, and allergies. The evidence for an infectious origin is mainly that cases have sometimes seemed to cluster in families, workplaces, and communities; but the U.S. Centers for Disease Control and Prevention (CDC) in Atlanta, Georgia, has concluded that CFS is not contagious.

Some studies also show that the disease may be linked to a kind of low blood pressure called *neurally meditated hypotension*—the hypotension is not thought to be a cause of CFS nor CFS of the hypotension, but the symptoms overlap considerably.

Incidence: Although people of all ages may get CFS, it mostly occurs in those between 22 and 44 years old. More than twice as many women as men have the condition. Based on several studies of CFS in cities, the Centers for Disease Control estimates that perhaps as many as half a million Americans meet the criteria for CFS.

Noticeable symptoms: Not surprisingly, given its official name, the primary symptom of CFS is extreme fatigue or tiredness. This fatigue is so severe that it can interfere with carrying on most usual activities. The feeling of fatigue is also made more intense by exercise, even mild exertion.

Some people with CFS may also develop a recurring sore throat without a discharge and other symptoms that usually go along with the flu. They may have aches and pains in muscles and joints, but in these cases the joints are not swollen or red. Other symptoms are painful lymph nodes in the armpits and neck, headaches, a slight fever, from 99.5°F to 100.5°F, and chills.

People with CFS may also experience the symptoms of depression. They may become confused and irritable and find themselves forgetting things. Typically, short-term memory is affected, but other types of memory impairment, such as absent-mindedness or inability to recall names, is usually not seen.

Despite the extreme fatigue, people with CFS may also have difficulty sleeping; and when sleep does occur, it may not eliminate fatigue.

Diagnosis: Your physician will want to determine the length of time over which you have experienced the symptoms listed above. By the official criteria for CFS from the Centers for Disease Control, such fatigue must have had a specific onset and then lasted for at least six months. All other diseases that cause chronic fatigue must be eliminated, including tuberculosis, cancer, anemia, diabetes, infection, heart disease, and AIDS. In order to eliminate these other diseases, the physician will perform a series of standard medical tests, such as blood tests and x-rays. Finally, there must be four or more symptoms from the following list:

- constant fatigue
- substantial impairment of short-term memory or noticeable inability to concentrate
- sore throat
- tender lymph nodes
- pain in the muscles
- pain in more than one joint unaccompanied by redness or swelling
- headaches that are different from those previously experienced
- fatigue on awakening after several hours' sleep
- feeling bad after exercise if that feeling lasts for more than a day

All of these must also have lasted for six months or more and have originated at the same time as the onset of chronic fatigue. Physicians also look for a recent acute infection or high stress that may have triggered the syndrome.

The criteria also reject CFS as a diagnosis when such conditions as hypothyroidism, sleep apnea, narcolepsy, mental illness (including anorexia or bulimia), alcoholism, substance abuse, and even severe obesity occur at the same time.

Treatment options: Just as the cause of CFS has not been determined, no cure has yet been found. In order to make the condition as easy as possible to live with, eat a well-balanced diet, get plenty of rest, and avoid stressful situations and extreme physical exertion. If your symptoms include muscle and joint pains and headaches, you may also take over-the-counter pain relievers. Some people find that avoiding foods with preservatives, dyes, and caffeine alleviates the symptoms.

Physicians have helped people overcome the depression or anxiety that accompanies CFS with antidepressants or with medicines that reduce panic attacks.

Neurally mediated hypotension, if found, may be treated with a diet that is high in salt and water consumption and with medications that raise or steady blood pressure.

Stages and progress: While there is no cure for CFS, it sometimes does go away spontaneously. That is, about half the people with the disease find their symptoms disappear within five years. Others have the symptoms decrease substantially, so that the disease no longer is as likely to interfere with their daily lives. However, for some people the symptoms may recur in full strength periodically over many years.

History: CFS is not a new disease, although it was first officially defined by the Centers for Disease Control in 1987. The symptoms have been reported in medical literature for over 200 years. The wide variety of symptoms has made it very difficult to separate CFS from other ailments. For many years it was thought that this syndrome was caused by the same virus that causes mononucleosis. But not everyone with CFS has been exposed to the virus that causes mononucleosis. Before the CDC sanctioned chronic fatigue syndrome as a specific physical ailment, some physicians had concluded that the syndrome was psychosomatic—caused by the mind instead of a disease of the body.

In 1985 two doctors in California, near Lake Tahoe, realized that they had a significant number of patients who experienced similar symptoms of fatigue so severe that it became completely disabling. Their work led to the official definition, and the number of cases seems to have grown dramatically since then.

Circulatory system

BODY SYSTEM

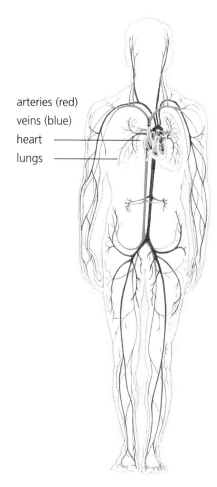

arteries (red)
veins (blue)
heart
lungs

Blood flows from heart to lungs, where it exchanges carbon dioxide for oxygen. The heart then pumps it through the body.

The circulatory system—often called the *vascular* (VAAS-kyuh-luhr) *system* by physicians—is the transport network that carries chemicals and some cells around the body. Its main parts have separate entries in these volumes.

General description: Blood is carried throughout the body in a closed system of tubes known collectively as *blood vessels.* Vessels carrying blood away from the heart are called arteries. The smallest arteries are called *arterioles* (ahr-TIHR-ee-OHLS). Arterioles merge into very tiny tubes called capillaries, whose walls are so thin that oxygen and nutrients pass through to reach cells. Meanwhile carbon dioxide and wastes from the cells pass through into the blood. The waste-carrying blood then enters veins, vessels that lead back to the heart.

An important side loop for the circulatory system pumps blood from the heart to the lungs to pick up fresh oxygen and to release accumulated carbon dioxide. After blood has made the trip to the lungs and back, it is directed into the first loop that passes through the rest of the body. Therefore the lungs, heart, and blood vessels may be thought of as a single body system of which the circulatory system is just a part.

Role: Although the primary function of the circulatory system is the transport of oxygen and carbon dioxide, much else is carried along with the blood—energy supplies for cells, water, hormones, minerals, immune system cells and substances, and other necessary materials. The materials include fats and cholesterol needed for building and maintaining cell membranes. Rarely, the blood carries undesirable bacteria, protozoa, or toxins.

Conditions that affect the circulatory system: Any condition or event that halts blood flow soon results in death to the cells that are no longer receiving blood. Dead tissue may deteriorate rapidly, a condition called gangrene. If a vital organ is affected, the interference with blood flow can be fatal. Flow may be blocked or diverted.

The most common way that blood flow is blocked is through buildup of material within an artery, as in atherosclerosis or embolism.

Any break in the circulatory system diverts blood from where it is intended to go. Breaks that let blood flow out of the body may be caused by a wound, which if deep also permits blood to leak inside the body. Another cause of diversion of blood is the bursting of a weak spot on an artery. Weak spots usually balloon into an aneurysm before they burst.

Conditions that affect blood pressure, such as hypertension (high blood pressure), can lead to breaks and blockages in the circulatory system. Both types of diabetes mellitus and also tobacco smoking tend to reduce circulation, especially in the hands and feet (the *extremities*), more so when diabetes is combined with smoking. This kind of reduction is termed *peripheral vascular disease;* it can interfere with walking or even reduce blood supply so much that cells die and gangrene develops.

Often when circulation is impaired, blood is kept by the vital organs in the trunk and skull, leading to loss of blood supply to the extremities. This can occur for reasons ranging from loss of blood from the system to diseases that reduce blood flow.

Cirrhosis of the liver

(sih-ROH-sihs)

DISEASE

TYPE: CHEMICAL;
       MECHANICAL

Most often associated with alcoholism, cirrhosis slowly destroys the liver and its ability to carry out many important bodily functions. If the patient stops drinking alcohol, the disease's progress can often be halted; if damage is not too great, the liver may even regenerate. In recent years liver transplants have been performed to treat selected cases of advanced cirrhosis.

Cause: Alcoholism is the most common cause of cirrhosis in the United States, but other agents may also induce the disease. These include toxic chemicals other than alcohol, reactions to drugs (prescription or illegal street), congestive heart failure, certain parasites, chronic liver infection (hepatitis), and even malnutrition. Some inherited diseases also cause cirrhosis.

An obstruction or infection of the liver's bile ducts causes a form of the disease called *biliary* (BIHL-ee-ehr-ee) *cirrhosis*. A rare condition, *primary biliary cirrhosis*, usually occurs in middle-aged women. No infection or obstruction is involved.

Phone doctor

Incidence: The eleventh leading cause of death in the United States, cirrhosis can be traced to alcohol-related problems in about 45% of the cases. Experts estimate that just over 9 people per 100,000 die of the disease each year.

Noticeable symptoms: Very early signs of cirrhosis can be hard to detect, since the disease may begin with general weakness and weight loss. Later symptoms, such as loss of appetite, indigestion, nausea, vomiting, abdominal swelling, intense itching, and a general feeling of ill health, become more noticeable. Cirrhosis patients may get *spider nevi*—spidery red marks—on the upper body, arms, and face. The lack of bile in the digestive system leads to light-colored stools. People with cirrhosis may also begin to bruise and bleed more easily as the disease progresses, since the liver manufactures vital clotting components.

Blockage of the portal vein that carries blood from the rest of the digestive system through the liver causes *hypertension* in the veins of the digestive system; the hypertension can cause distended veins called *varices* (VEHR-uh-SEEZ) in the esophagus and stomach. Such veins often break open, causing profuse bleeding that is a recognizable symptom of cirrhosis.

Cirrhosis is a life-threatening disease. If you or someone in your family experiences the symptoms above, get prompt medical attention.

Diagnosis: A doctor may be able to diagnose cirrhosis based on a patient's past history and a physical examination. But it will be important to determine the primary cause and extent of the liver damage. Blood tests, a liver biopsy (tissue sample), endoscopy to look for varices, ultrasound, and computerized tomography (CT) scans are all employed. The small piece of liver removed during a biopsy will show the extent of the tissue damage. Ultrasound and CT scans provide information on changes in liver size, tumors, and other factors relating to cirrhosis.

Treatment options: Although liver tissue can regenerate, the widespread damage caused by advanced cirrhosis cannot be reversed. Medical treatment can help prevent further damage and maintain liver function at its current level.

Removing the primary cause of the liver damage is the doctor's first priority. Whether cirrhosis was alcohol-induced

12-Step meeting

or not, drinking must be given up completely. Alcoholics may need the help of a support group such as Alcoholic Anonymous. Adhering to a well-balanced, nutritious diet high in carbohydrates and vitamins and low in fat is also important.

Among the medications the doctor may prescribe are antacids to deal with abdominal discomfort, diuretics to reduce fluid buildup, and, in certain types of cirrhosis, corticosteroids or other immune-system-suppressing drugs. Where there are problems with bleeding, blood transfusions will replace lost blood volume.

People with advanced cirrhosis, especially that caused by chronic hepatitis and primary biliary cirrhosis, may be candidates for the most drastic treatment, a liver transplant. Medical experts report that 80% of transplant patients now survive for five or more years after the operation.

Stages and progress: A healthy liver performs several important bodily functions. It helps controls the volume of blood in the body; produces substances needed to make blood clot; regulates fluid amount and chemical balances in blood; neutralizes toxins absorbed by the intestines; and helps convert nutrients in food into a source of energy. But heavy drinking, toxic chemicals, hepatitis, and other agents slowly damage liver tissue. Cirrhosis occurs when enough healthy tissue has been damaged and replaced by scar tissue and fat. The liver simply does not have enough tissue left to perform its vital tasks.

Once the disease reaches its later stages, the patient may begin suffering jaundice, a symptom of liver disease and some other conditions. The skin and whites of the eyes turn a yellowish color. Men lose interest in sex and become impotent, and may develop painfully swollen breasts. Women may stop having their menstrual periods. Fluid builds up in the abdomen and ankles, and the likelihood of bleeding in the esophagus and stomach increases. Liver cancer may develop. Severe bleeding in advanced cases may finally cause death. Complete liver failure is also fatal.

Meanwhile, the decline in liver function also affects the patient's mental state. Irritability, an inability to concentrate, and trembling of the hands all become more noticeable. Later the patient's memory will be impaired. Confusion, delirium, and drowsiness in later stages indicate liver failure.

Avoid alcohol

Prevention: Anyone who drinks heavily or suffers alcohol addiction risks developing cirrhosis. Whether there are signs of cirrhosis or not, doctors generally urge people with alcohol addiction to seek help and caution heavy drinkers to cut back. Once cirrhosis has developed, no matter what the cause, the patient should stop drinking alcohol altogether. Continued drinking with cirrhosis almost certainly leads to liver failure and death.

Claudication

See **Leg cramps**

Cleft lip and palate

DISORDER

TYPE: DEVELOPMENTAL

See also
**Childbirth, complications of
Genetic diseases**

The facial features take shape in the early weeks of prenatal development. Parts of the face are formed separately and then join, or fuse, together. Sometimes this process fails to be fully completed, especially in the area of the mouth. The result is a *cleft* (gap) in the upper lip, in the hard palate (the bony roof of the mouth), the soft palate (the area behind the roof of the mouth), or in some combination of these. A cleft lip is sometimes known as *harelip*.

Cause: The causes of cleft lip and cleft palate are unknown. The conditions are familial (they tend to run in families), and they occur more often in certain ethnic groups. But they have no clear pattern of inheritance, so are not considered entirely genetic in origin.

Cleft lip and cleft palate may also accompany a wide range of other birth-defect syndromes, some of which are clearly genetic.

Incidence: The most common form of this group of birth defects is a combination of cleft lip and cleft palate, which occurs in about one in a thousand babies.

Noticeable symptoms: Both conditions are clearly evident at birth. Feeding may be difficult for an infant with cleft lip or palate.

Diagnosis: A pediatrician will examine the baby carefully to ascertain the extent of the cleft or clefts and to determine whether they are signs of other birth-defect syndromes.

Treatment: Cleft lip and cleft palate can be remedied by surgery, and modern techniques are quite effective in concealing signs of malformation. Surgery for cleft lip is usually performed in early infancy and for cleft palate between nine and eighteen months.

Prevention: Evidence suggests that pregnant women can reduce the risk of cleft lip and palate in their babies by not smoking or drinking and by making sure they get enough vitamins, particularly folic acid. Although there is a genetic component to cleft lip and palate, the presence of the disorder in one child does not appreciably increase the risk for the same disorder in later children of the same parents.

Outlook: Most clefts have only cosmetic effects. Surgical repair is usually a complete remedy. A severe cleft palate may cause feeding and speech difficulties, dental malformations, or partial loss of hearing, any of which may need special care.

Clinical depression

DISEASE

TYPE: MENTAL; CHEMICAL

See also
Alcoholism
Bipolar disorder
Drug abuse
Mental illnesses
Paranoia
SAD (seasonal affective disorder)

Everyone feels discouraged from time to time. Many people report "having the blues" or the "blahs." Few of us get through life without experiencing depression of this sort at one time or another. Clinical depression—also known as *major depression* or *serious depression*—however, is more than just feeling sad or down. Although stemming from chemical imbalances in the brain, clinical depression is a "whole-body" illness that affects the body as well as the mind.

There are two basic types of major depression. Depressive episodes can occur alone or can alternate with episodes of excitement called *manic* behavior. In the latter case the illness is not clinical depression, and it responds to different medications from those used for clinical depression. The alternating manic-depressive illness is called bipolar disorder, and it is discussed as a separate entry. A somewhat milder depression that tends to come each winter is called SAD (seasonal affective disorder).

Cause: Clinical depression may start without a clear reason, or it may begin with ordinary depression caused by specific events. Many women become temporarily depressed in the weeks following childbirth; this is called *postpartum depression*. Other medical events that can trigger depression include heart surgery, such as a bypass operation. There is some evidence that AIDS is often accompanied by clinical depression that goes beyond distress over the disease itself. Depression can be caused as a side effect of some drugs, including blood pressure medications, antihistamines, and steroids; this depression is most easily cured, since removing or adjusting the dose of the drug usually solves the problem.

Researchers have learned that clinical depression results from complex interactions among brain chemicals. The exact origin of impaired chemical interactions is unknown at this time, but there is probably a genetic component. Depression seems to occur more often in conjunction with alcoholism and drug abuse; this may result from a hereditary complex that includes genes predisposing one toward addiction in general and toward depression.

Incidence: Depression is America's number-one mental health problem. The Centers for Disease Control and Prevention estimates that about 4 to 5% of the population in the United States suffer from major depression at any given time—almost 15 million Americans. Fewer than 2% of depressed people are properly diagnosed or receive treatment. Depression may be partly influenced by industrialization: Clinical depression rates have risen in most developed countries that have been studied.

People in every age group, from children to the elderly, can develop clinical depression, but because of rising rates younger people are more likely to have experienced it than their older counterparts. Twice as many women as men are affected. Over a full lifetime about 20 to 26% of women have depressive episodes, while only 8 to 12% of men do. (These figures include bipolar disorder, which accounts for somewhere between 10 to 20% of all major depression.)

Noticeable symptoms: If you are clinically depressed, you may notice three kinds of symptoms:

Emotional: You may have a feeling of great sadness and hopelessness and lose interest in the people and activities around you. You may feel and express guilt and pessimism, and may not be able to see the good side of anything. Your outlook on life will be bleak. In addition, you may feel empty and be having crying spells. These symptoms often have little or nothing to do with the actual events around you.

Behavioral: You may be irritable, find that your memory is poor, and be unable to concentrate.

Physical: You may experience a loss of appetite, weight loss or gain, headaches, and trouble with sleeping.

If these feelings persist for two weeks or more, you may even find yourself contemplating suicide. ***If you feel suicidal, seek medical assistance immediately. Most phone books contain listings for local suicide or crisis centers.*** Clearly, you need help to cope with the depression that is overwhelming you. Some 2 to 8% of patients with depression do commit suicide each year.

In some cases depression produces symptoms of psychosis, such as hallucinations or paranoia.

The progress of clinical depression differs greatly. Some people have only one episode during a lifetime, while others have repeated incidents. In some people an episode lasts a few weeks; in others it lasts for months or years.

Diagnosis: Mental illnesses are diagnosed according to specific criteria. Your physician will look for five or more of the following symptoms that have persisted for more than two weeks:

- persistent low, anxious, or empty feelings
- decreased energy, fatigue, a feeling of being slowed down
- loss of interest or pleasure in usual activities, including sex
- insomnia, early morning waking, oversleeping, or other sleep disturbances
- appetite change or weight change (either loss or gain)
- feelings of hopelessness or pessimism
- feelings of guilt, worthlessness, or helplessness
- thoughts of death or suicide
- difficulty in concentrating, remembering, or making decisions
- chronic aches or pains without physical origin

Since there are many diseases that can cause depression, your doctor will want to check you carefully to rule them out. Since some prescription drugs can trigger depression, tell your physician about every medication you take.

Treatment options: The National Institute of Mental Health estimates that more than 80% of those who suffer depression

Phone doctor

can be helped by appropriate treatment, although perhaps half will have another episode at a later time.

The major treatments for depression are antidepressive medication, psychotherapy, and a combination of the two.

Unlike psychoactive drugs that are sometimes used to treat other forms of mental illness, the newest antidepressants, of which the most common is fluoxetine (trade name: Prozac; related drugs are Zoloft and Paxil), usually cause only mild and temporary side effects. They are not habit forming, but people who take them should be carefully monitored to make sure that they are getting the correct dose. Often these drugs take several weeks to be effective. High alcohol intake, while probably not the cause of depression, makes symptoms worse and should be avoided during treatment.

Prozac and related drugs work by changing the way that the brain handles a neurotransmitter called *serotonin*, so these are known as selective serotonin reuptake inhibitors. Other drugs used as antidepressants include the tricyclic antidepressants (trade names include Elavil and Tofranil) along with various drugs that have some antidepressant activity or that are antipsychotics.

Psychotherapy can help reorient a person whose life and relationships have been altered by clinical depression. Most studies show that a combination of drug therapy and psychotherapy works better than either alone.

If other treatments fail, electroconvulsive therapy (ECT), also known as shock treatment, is effective in more than three-quarters of the patients on whom it is used. ECT is often accompanied by memory loss but appears to have no other side effects.

Prevention: If you begin to feel depressed, there are some steps you can take that may help. Avoid alcohol, which is a potent depressant. Stop taking drugs other than those prescribed by a physician—and tell your physician that you are depressed. Regular exercise helps some people. Light, especially sunlight, may also help. Avoid making major decisions while you are depressed. Make a plan for activity, and stay involved with others. These changes, activities, and a few days' time usually help ordinary depression. *If symptoms of depression last longer than two weeks, see your doctor or a psychological counselor.*

Avoid alcohol

Phone doctor

Exercise

Depression and the artist

We often know about the clinical depression of authors because they have written about it, sometimes in poetry or fiction, sometimes in memoirs. Many of the artists who suffered from depression eventually committed suicide. Among the best known are Ernest Hemingway and Sylvia Plath.

Others managed to survive this often deadly disease. One such survivor is William Styron, author of *Confessions of Nat Turner* and *Sophie's Choice,* among other celebrated novels. As Styron reached 60, at the height of his fame and success, he stumbled into deep depression. He recognized that he had a disease and sought medical assistance. Just at the edge of suicide, already arranging a will and suicide note, a familiar piece of music lifted his spirits for a moment.

He called his doctor and reported how near he was to suicide. Styron was hospitalized and his medication adjusted. Soon, ending a year of terror and sleeplessness, his old self began to return. Finished with his depression at last, he wrote a short book, *Darkness Visible: A Memoir of Madness,* in the hope of helping others become aware of the symptoms and of the need for help.

History: For many centuries clinical depression has been misdiagnosed. It was often dismissed as hysteria and treated, if at all, with "nerve tonics." The prevailing opinion was that depression was a personal weakness, and patients were urged to "snap out of it." Chemical studies of the brain and successful treatment with medicines that alter levels of brain chemicals have demonstrated, however, that depression is not a result of personal weakness or a condition that can be willed or wished out of existence.

Depression fuels rising teen suicide rates

High school and college-aged people suffer high rates of clinical depression. Many parents and teachers do not recognize the illness because its symptoms may look to them like normal teenage problems. Some of these symptoms are abrupt mood swings, irritability, taking of inappropriate risks, and troubles with friends, teachers, and parents.

If left undiagnosed and untreated, young people with severe clinical depression may resort to suicide. In fact, suicide is now the second leading cause of death among people between the ages of 15 and 24. Three out of four suicides by teens have been preceded by unsuccessful suicide attempts or threats. Researchers urge us to take threats of suicide seriously; they are cries for help. Most cities have suicide-prevention hot lines available by telephone; listings for them can be found in the phone directory. Sometimes these are listed as crisis-intervention hot lines.

Clubfoot and related problems

DISORDER

TYPE: DEVELOPMENTAL

See also
Childbirth, complications of
Foot problems

Among the most common birth defects are deformities of the feet. They may occur in one or both feet and can eventually cause walking difficulties that range from almost unnoticeable to severely crippling. Three of these conditions are especially prevalent.

■ *Clubfoot,* technically known as *equinovarus* (EH-kwiy-noh-VAY-ruhs), is the most serious. The foot is twisted inward and downward, and the condition will not improve with time. If it is not successfully treated, the afflicted child will not be able to place the sole flat on the ground but will have to walk on the ball or the side of the foot. Normal growth is also hindered. If just one foot is affected, that foot will be smaller than the other, and the leg will be shorter.

■ *Calcaneus valgus* (caal-CAY-nee-uhs VAAL-guhs) is the most common of these defects. The affected foot is angled upward and outward. The condition is relatively mild and usually goes away by itself. Otherwise it may eventually cause the child to walk on the heel or the inner side of the foot.

■ *Metatarsus varus* or *adductus* (MEHT-uh-TAAR-suhs VAAR-uhs or ah-DUK-tuhs) is also relatively mild and generally resolves itself over time. The front of the affected foot turns inward; this may eventually cause awkwardness in walking or running.

Cause: Calcaneus valgus and metatarsus adductus are considered to be *deformations* that occur during later prenatal development. That is, one or both feet get cramped and twisted in a constricted uterus. Clubfoot, on the other hand, is thought to be a *malformation* of early development in which the tendons and ligaments of the foot and ankle fail to form properly. Clubfoot tends to appear more often in certain families but is not clearly genetic.

Incidence: All these defects are fairly common. Clubfoot occurs in about 1 in 750 babies, metatarsus adductus in about 1 in 500, and calcaneus valgus a little more often.

Noticeable symptoms: These defects are usually visible at birth.

Diagnosis: X-rays and other special tests may be used to determine the nature and severity of the defects.

Treatment: Mild defects may merit no other care than careful monitoring until they disappear by themselves. More severe defects may require remedial treatment, starting soon after birth, so that the baby will not have difficulties when beginning to walk.

Stretching. Calcaneus valgus and metatarsus adductus can sometimes be corrected by simple stretching exercises performed by a parent.

Casts. The most common treatment for foot deformities is to manipulate the foot into the most normal position possible without causing pain and then to apply a plaster cast to hold the foot immobile in that position. The process is repeated every two weeks or so until the position is normal. Then a splint is used to preserve the change.

Surgery. Severe clubfoot may require surgery to repair the defective tendons and ligaments.

Outlook: Once even a severe foot deformity is treated, the child can usually walk normally.

Cluster headaches

DISEASE

TYPE: COMBINATION

See also
Headache
Migraine
Pain

Cluster headaches take their name from their characteristic pattern of occurrence. Attacks are concentrated in periodic clusters, usually from one to three times a day for one to two months. These clusters are followed by periods of remission that last anywhere from several months to several years. Some persons, however, experience daily headaches for as long as a year.

Attacks come on suddenly and without warning. They last from half an hour to two hours and then quickly subside. They tend to be repeated at the same times each day and often occur at night. The headaches affect only one side of the head, usually in the area nearest the eye. Sufferers describe the pain as excruciatingly intense.

Attacks may be accompanied by other symptoms. In particular, the eye on the affected side may become red and gush tears, the eyelid may droop, and the nose may become clogged with mucus.

Most cluster headaches are *episodic;* the clusters alternate with periods of remission. In a minority of cases the condition becomes *chronic*, with little or no relief between daily attacks. Each of these two forms can switch to the other.

Cause: The cause of cluster headaches is unknown. They were once thought to be closely related to migraine but now appear to be a separate disorder. Current research suggests that they have their source in the central nervous system and may be triggered by the faulty functioning of *neurotransmitters,* chemicals that transmit impulses from one nerve cell to another. One neurotransmitter in particular, serotonin, is believed to play a major role.

Incidence: Cluster headaches are uncommon but not rare. By one estimate about 1 in 1,450 people suffer from them. Men are five to six times more likely than women to be affected.

Noticeable symptoms: The clustered attacks of intense pain, occurring on just one side of the head at about the same times each day, are unmistakable.

Diagnosis: There are no special tests for cluster headaches. They are generally diagnosed from symptoms reported by the sufferer, supplemented by observation of related effects such as a red, teary eye with a drooping eyelid.

Treatment: Symptomatic treatment aims to relieve pain during an attack and to cut the attack short. Since attacks come with little or no warning, ordinary painkillers, even opioids such as codeine, are ineffective, in large part because they take effect too slowly. The most widely used drugs are those that regulate the function of serotonin, such as sumatriptan, which can be self-injected, and ergotamine, which can be inhaled. Inhaling pure oxygen is also effective.

Prevention: Regular and restful sleep helps reduce attacks. Also, since most people who suffer these headaches drink alcohol and smoke tobacco, it is thought that stopping both habits—a good idea for other reasons as well—can help. Sometimes a particular food appears to trigger an attack.

The corticosteroid prednisone, sometimes combined with ergotamine, is the most common drug used to prevent attacks. Other drugs include methysergide, a chemical relative of ergotamine, and verapamil, a calcium channel blocker used in the treatment of hypertension and heart disease. For chronic cluster headaches compounds of lithium, also used to treat bipolar disorder, appear to be especially effective. Both prednisone and lithium can have undesirable side effects and must be monitored carefully by a physician.

Outlook: Once they begin, cycles of cluster headaches tend to persist throughout life. In many cases, however, treatment can substantially reduce the intensity and frequency of attacks.

Cold sore

DISEASE

TYPE: INFECTIOUS (VIRAL)

See also
Canker
Chicken pox
Genital herpes
Shingles
Viruses and disease

Small sores that develop on the lips or within the mouth may be cold sores, also called *fever blisters*. Cold sores are highly contagious and should not be confused with cankers, which are not contagious. Sores of any type, as well as wounds, are also called *lesions* (LEE-zhuhnz).

Cause: A virus known as *Herpes simplex* causes cold sores. Usually, cold sores result from the herpes type I strain, which is slightly different than the type II strain, which causes genital herpes. The herpes family of viruses also causes chicken pox and shingles.

One can become infected with herpes type I by kissing or otherwise touching another person's cold sore. Infection can also result from using utensils, cups, towels, or other objects that have been contaminated by contact with a cold sore. *Avoid touching the sore and then touching your eye; this can cause a serious infection that untreated can lead to loss of sight in the eye.*

Once infected, certain stimuli can initiate blister formation, including stress, bright sunlight, or other infections.

Incidence: Cold sores are very common. Once you become infected with viruses from the herpes family, they stay with you for life. The viruses apparently reside in nerve cells, remaining dormant until something causes them to form lesions. Stress, food allergies, sun exposure, fever, and the start of a menstrual period often act as triggers.

Noticeable symptoms: Cold sores almost always develop on or near the lips, though they can form inside the mouth or even in the nostrils or on eyelids. The first symptom is a painful tingling. Within several days one or more blisters appear. They are round, reddish, and filled with pus. They break and ooze, then form a yellowish crust. The blisters usually heal within a week.

If a fever or swollen lymph nodes develop, see your doctor. Also see the doctor if you have frequent outbreaks or if the sores are numerous and severe.

Treatment options: Nonprescription ointments containing benzocaine can be applied to cold sores to numb the pain. Painkillers such as aspirin also may help. A doctor may prescribe acyclovir ointment to prevent the viruses from reproducing. Applying acyclovir ointment or taking the oral form at the first sign of tingling may stop blisters from forming or at least reduce their severity. If bright sun is a trigger, a sunblock on the lips when at the beach or skiing can help.

Phone doctor

Colic

(KOL-ihk)

SYMPTOM

See also
Cramp
Gallstones
Infants and disease
Kidney and bladder stones
Lead poisoning
Menstrual pain

Colic in common speech refers to an attack of abdominal pain in infants. However, physicians may use the term in conjunction with other conditions that produce abdominal pain. For example, *biliary colic* is pain caused by a gallstone stuck in the bile duct. Women who suffer abdominal pain during their periods have *menstrual colic,* commonly called cramps. *Lead colic* is a symptom of lead poisoning, once common among painters working with lead-based paint and at one time caused by drinking beverages produced in stills or cider presses that were constructed with lead linings. *Renal colic* is caused by a kidney stone, either in the kidney or the duct leading from it, the ureter.

Parts affected: Infant colic is caused by spasmodic contractions of a baby's intestines. The condition occurs in one out of five babies, usually during the infant's first three or four months.

Cause: Doctors are not sure why some babies get colic. Possible explanations include an immature digestive system, overfeeding or too fast feeding, swallowing of air during feeding, allergy to milk, or even the baby's awareness of parental anxiety.

Related symptoms: Infants with colic usually turn red-faced and cry loudly, often pulling their knees up to the chest, clenching fists, and scowling. Usually the attacks come at about the same time each day and may continue for hours.

Relief of symptoms: Other than easing parents' anxiety by eliminating more dangerous disorders as the cause of colic attacks, doctors can do little to improve the situation of infant colic. Babies usually remain healthy despite bouts of colic. Often physicians suggest changing an infant's diet in some way, but this may be more important in letting parents feel that they are trying to help than in actually eliminating the symptom. Taking steps to keep the baby calm or quietly entertained and making sure that the infant is not hungry can sometimes help. Colic usually clears up by itself by the baby's fourth month.

Colitis

(kuh-LIY-tuhs)

DISEASE

TYPE: AUTOIMMUNE; GENETIC

Phone doctor

People who experience abdominal pain accompanied by bloody diarrhea may have colitis, an inflammation of the colon or of the entire large intestine. This disease is potentially very serious.

Cause: Colitis usually refers to *ulcerative colitis,* the cause of which is uncertain—there is a genetic component, and it also is classed as an autoimmune disease. Ulcerative colitis is marked by lesions (sores, also called *ulcers*) of the mucous membrane that lines the large intestine.

Noticeable symptoms: Colitis is typically accompanied by high fever, sharp pains in the lower abdomen, and frequent diarrhea. Stools smell foul and often contain blood, mucus, and pus, or may be tarry from internal bleeding. Sometimes the stools seem to consist mainly of bloody water. Weight loss, fatigue, and joint pain may occur. *Because the disease can develop rapidly and become life-threatening, see a doctor as soon as possible.*

Diagnosis: An instrument called a *colonoscope* will be inserted into the large intestine to examine its walls. A tissue sample may be taken and examined under a microscope to rule out cancer. X-rays may be taken.

Treatment options: Small meals and high liquid intake along with sources of electrolytes (such as bananas—high in potassium) often help reduce symptoms. The basic medical treatment consists of antibiotics and anti-inflammatory drugs to control the disease and to prevent new flareups. Suppression of the immune system has been tried in difficult cases.

Acute attacks may require hospitalization. In severe cases surgery to remove the colon is employed; this halts the disease, but requires changes in lifestyle that many find difficult to accept.

Stages and progress: Often the first attack of colitis is the worst. Thereafter a pattern of flareups alternating with periods of remission may develop. Other parts of the body may become involved. For example, joints—especially those of the wrists, knees, and ankles—may become inflamed, and the flow of bile from the liver may be obstructed. People who have ulcerative colitis for ten years or longer have an increased risk of developing cancer of the colon.

Colon and rectal cancers

DISEASE

TYPE: CANCER

Colon cancer and rectal cancer are diseases of the large intestine. They also are called *colorectal* (KOH-luh-REHK-tuhl) *cancer*. Many cases begin as small growths, called polyps, that eventually become cancerous. Medical procedures can detect and remove polyps in their precancerous stage. If colon or rectal cancers are detected and treated in their early stages, they are highly curable.

Parts affected: Colon or rectal cancers develop in the large intestine, which is the final portion of the digestive tract. The main part of the large intestine is called the *colon*. It opens into a short section called the *rectum*, which leads to the *anus*.

Cause: Several factors appear to increase a person's chances of developing colon or rectal cancers. These include a family history of polyps, colorectal cancers, or other cancers. A personal history of polyps or other cancers also may indicate a greater likelihood of colorectal cancer. Inflammatory bowel diseases, such as colitis and Crohn's disease, may develop into colon or rectal cancer. Diet may be a contributory cause; people whose diets are low in fiber, fruits, and vegetables appear to have an increased susceptibility to colon or rectal cancers. Physical inactivity, use of tobacco, and exposure to certain chemicals, including asbestos, have also been linked to the disease. A few people have genetic diseases that tend to produce colorectal cancers; the same genes make other forms of cancer more likely as well.

Incidence: Each year approximately 135,000 Americans are diagnosed with colon or rectal cancers. An estimated 57,000 people die from these diseases, accounting for about 10% of annual cancer deaths.

Noticeable symptoms: Often there are no early symptoms, so frequent testing is necessary in older persons (see Prevention and possible actions below). A change in bowel habits that lasts more than a few days, bleeding from the rectum, blood in the stool, and cramps or constant abdominal pain may indicate the presence of a tumor. *If you experience any of these symptoms, see a doctor as soon as possible.*

Diagnosis: The physician will feel the abdomen and lymph nodes for signs of a mass or swelling. Blood and urine samples will be taken and checked for chemical abnormalities. A sigmoidoscopy or colonoscopy will be performed. In these procedures the inner walls of the large intestine are examined with a lighted tube inserted through the anus. Tissue is removed from polyps and other abnormal growths and examined under a microscope to determine if it is cancerous.

Stages and progress: Determining the stage of a cancer enables a physician to choose the most effective treatment. Staging describes the size of the tumor and whether it has spread to other organs. A widely used system assigns a stage of I, II, III, or IV. I is an early stage, with no indication that the cancer has spread beyond the colon or rectum. IV is the most advanced stage, with the cancer having spread, or *metastasized*, to distant parts of the body. Cancers caught early can nearly always be cured.

Treatment options: Surgery to remove the tumor is the most common treatment for colorectal cancers. It is seldom necessary to remove large portions of the colon. Chemotherapy and

Phone doctor

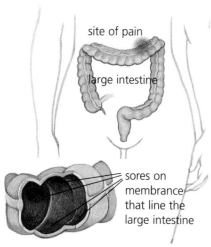

site of pain

large intestine

sores on membrane that line the large intestine

Colonoscopy
Examination of the inner walls of the large intestine is conducted with a lighted tube inserted through the anus, usually in a hospital or well-equipped specialist's office. The same instrument is often equipped with a device that can remove a small portion of diseased walls for further testing.

radiation may also be used if the cancer has grown through the outer wall of the intestine or spread to the lymph nodes.

Experimental vaccines given to patients in early stages of colon cancer show promise. Patients with early-stage cancers who received the vaccines improved their chances of remaining cancer-free. Some of the vaccines are synthetic; others are custom-made from a patient's own cancer cells.

Prevention and possible actions: A diet high in fiber, fruits, and vegetables and low in fat appears to reduce the risk of colon or rectal cancers. Some evidence indicates that non-steroidal anti-inflammatory drugs (NSAIDS) such as aspirin also may reduce risk.

Early detection is key to the successful treatment of colon or rectal cancers. Adults age 50 and older who are at average risk are advised to have a fecal occult blood test, which looks for traces of blood in feces, every year. Those over 50 should also have a sigmoidoscopy every five years or a colonoscopy every ten years. People at increased risk, perhaps because of a family history of colon or rectal cancers, generally are advised to begin screening at an earlier age and to be tested more frequently.

High fiber

Coma

(KOH-muh)

Coma is unconsciousness from which, unlike sleep, one cannot be aroused.

Part affected: The brain requires a great deal of oxygen to function, and loss of oxygen supply from any region, or from clogging of the arteries or shock, can result in coma. When coma lasts for a long time, inactivity can result in muscle atrophy (wasting away and loss of power) or in bedsores (ulcers caused by lying in the same position for long periods of time).

Related symptoms: The individual lacks any movement of the eyes and does not awake in response to sound or touch or shaking. There is even no response to pain.

Associations: Coma is a common result of various types of damage to the brain. These include physical injury from falls or blows or from the pressure of a brain tumor, aneurysm, or blood clot.

Poisoning, including drug and alcohol overdose, can also induce coma. A particularly potent combination includes alcohol taken in conjunction with other drugs. Some bacterial or viral illnesses attack the brain, causing inflammation that leads to coma.

Type 1 diabetes can induce coma, commonly called *diabetic coma* or *ketosis* (kee-TOH-suhs), by altering blood chemistry so that the blood becomes, in effect, a brain poison.

Electrolyte imbalance, which is most often caused by excessive sweating, can also cause coma. (Electrolytes, which are important cell messengers, are the sodium and potassium in the blood.)

Prevention: In many cases coma stems from risky behavior that results in physical damage or overdoses of drugs. A person with diabetes needs to monitor blood sugar, control diet, and use insulin as needed to avoid ketosis. Maintaining fluids in the body when working hard in hot weather is important as well.

Relief of symptoms: There is no treatment that is known to relieve coma unless the underlying cause is eliminated, such as relieving pressure on the brain or restoring balance to the blood supply.

Common cold

DISEASE

TYPE: INFECTIOUS (VIRAL)

See also
Allergies
Coughs
Fever
Hay fever
Influenza
Nose and throat conditions
Pneumonia
"Strep"
Viruses and disease

The common cold is a contagious and generally mild infection that causes inflammation of the mucous membranes lining the nose and throat. The resulting stuffy, runny nose and the occasional cough and sore throat that accompany the cold are the short-lived consequences of this inflammation. For these symptoms there is no cure except patience.

Cause: The common cold, also known as a *head cold*, is not one disease but a group of related syndromes brought on by any one of more than 200 different viruses. Of these the rhino (Greek for "nose") and corona (so named for their characteristic crownlike shape) viruses account for about half of all colds; six or more other types of virus are thought to cause the remainder.

Transmission: In order to infect an individual, a cold virus must gain entry to the mucous membranes that line the upper respiratory system. This transmission of viruses most often occurs via the hands, the infectious material passing from an infected individual directly to a healthy person via a handshake, for example; it may also travel indirectly via a hard surface that two individuals have touched—a doorknob, a telephone receiver, or a bathroom drinking glass.

When the uninfected person rubs his or her nose or eyes and touches the inside of the nose or the inner corners of the eyes, the virus finds its way to the membrane. There the virus is able to attach to and invade the underlying cells to cause infection. Uncovered sneezes that can project tiny virus-laden droplets into the air are a less frequent mode of travel for cold viruses.

Incidence: Young children, because they play in very close contact with each other and have not yet learned to practice simple routines for avoiding infections, are especially vulnerable to infection, with six to ten colds per year being the usual pattern. These same children then become the principal means of infecting their parents. As people age and experience cold after cold, however, they gradually develop a degree of immunity to scores of cold viruses. Young adults, for example, may have only two or three colds per year. But there are so many different viruses, and the level of immunity developed is so low, that almost no one ever gets to a point of total resistance.

Noticeable symptoms: While all colds share certain basic symptoms, these vary somewhat in severity according to the particular virus contracted. Classic symptoms—most of which arise as the result of the body trying to rid itself of the infection—include runny nose, cough, sore throat, sneezing, watery eyes, and hoarseness.

The common cold may easily be confused with other diseases. Should a high fever accompanied by overall body pain occur, the infection is more likely to be influenza, a more serious respiratory virus. An illness that includes difficulty in breathing and a persistent fever may be pneumonia, which requires medical attention. A very sore throat may be a streptococcal infection, which requires antibiotics.

Often what seems to be a cold at first will be limited to a runny nose, sneezing, and watery eyes; if it is not winter, and if the symptoms seem to come and go, the problem may be an allergy, especially hay fever, and not a cold at all.

Relief of symptoms: Medical science has no cure as yet for the common cold, and recommended treatments are designed to reduce symptoms only. If your throat feels dry, add moisture to the air with a vaporizer or humidifier. Drink lots of liquids; if there is pain, take acetaminophen at bedtime to aid sleep. Over-the-counter cold remedies may give a measure of relief to some, but they are typically combination remedies that contain more different medications than a particular cold may need. The extra substances may cause drowsiness or other unpleasant side effects. Antihistamines will suppress hay fever symptoms but have little or no effect on cold symptoms.

A physician should be consulted only if symptoms persist for more than a week or so, or suddenly worsen. In such instances a secondary bacterial infection may have developed for which treatment may be helpful or perhaps even necessary.

Prevention: Many people believe there are ways of preventing colds—by taking large quantities of vitamin C, by staying out of cold drafts, and by avoiding getting chilled or wet for prolonged periods, for example. Numerous experiments have been run in which volunteers submitted to weeks of misery to test these theories. But the only precaution that has been shown scientifically to work is frequent hand washing and keeping hands away from nose and eyes.

Wash hands

Although we think of colds as starting with a chill or draft, the virus that causes the disease is most commonly passed from person to person by touching or sneezing or by touching surfaces, such as playing cards, that have previously been touched or sneezed on by a person carrying the disease. Frequent hand washing is the best way to reduce the risk of catching the common cold.

Concussion

(kon-KUSH-uhn)

DISEASE

TYPE: INJURY

See also
Amnesia
Brain
Coma
Dizziness
Head injuries
Shaken baby syndrome

An accidental fall or a sharp blow to the head can cause a concussion, a minor injury that involves no permanent damage to the brain. A concussion can occur with or without a brief loss of consciousness.

Injuries involving the head are always potentially serious. Seek medical assistance whenever you feel dazed or after loss of consciousness because of a blow to the head.

Cause: The skull provides protection for the brain, absorbing most of the shock from minor bumps and moderate blows. But sometimes impact is so intense that the brain actually moves within its protective case. Severe shaking can also bounce the brain off the inside of the skull, especially in young children. The temporary loss of function of part of the brain from such a blow is called concussion.

Concussion can make the victim feel dazed or even lose consciousness. The brain is not permanently damaged, however. Apart from some minor discomfort most people recover completely from a concussion.

More serious types of head injury arise when the blow is hard enough to cause internal bleeding or to fracture the skull. The effects of internal bleeding may not show up at first, which is why all head injuries require attention by a physician.

Incidence: Overall, about 10 million head injuries are reported in the United States annually. About 80% of them are not serious enough to involve brain damage.

Noticeable symptoms: Dizziness or loss of consciousness is possible after being hit in the head. External cuts and bruises may be minor, though external injury cannot be used to determine whether more serious internal head injuries are present. Headache for a day or two and trouble concentrating are also possible. Vision may be somewhat blurred. Faintness and nausea are common, and even vomiting.

Loss of memory also may accompany a concussion. Usually incidents occurring just before and during the accident causing the concussion are forgotten. Sometimes, though, the temporary amnesia blocks out memories of a few weeks or more leading up to the accident. The memories do return in time, with the more distant ones usually coming back first.

Phone doctor

Remember that symptoms of more serious head injuries may not appear until hours or days after an accident. Because more serious head injury is always a possibility, *see your doctor right away when you are hit hard enough to become dazed or lose consciousness.*

Diagnosis: The doctor will look for outward symptoms of serious head injury, including dilation of a pupil in the eye, persistent confusion, difficulty in speaking, drowsiness, or an increasing feeling of tiredness. If further tests seem warranted, the doctor may order x-rays or a CT scan to be sure that the skull is not fractured or that there is no internal bleeding.

Avoid aspirin

Treatment options: While recovering from a concussion, avoid any vigorous movement that may jar the head. Also, put off doing anything that requires mental concentration. *Do not take aspirin after receiving a blow to the head, however. Aspirin may contribute to bleeding.*

Stages and progress: In most instances of mild concussion there is full recovery within a few days. But for about one-third of those who suffer concussions, certain symptoms may persist, including prolonged bouts with headache and dizziness. These patients may also experience irritability, inability to concentrate, restlessness, insomnia, moodiness, or even depression.

Even up to a month after a head injury the following symptoms are a signal to return to the physician: persistent drowsiness; difficulties in speech; paralysis of any part of the body; falling or other loss of coordination; noticeable personality changes or confusion; widening of the pupil in one eye more than the other; continued loss of memory; severe headache.

Congenital digestive system conditions

REFERENCE

Defects or illnesses that are present at birth are called *congenital*. The congenital disorders of the digestive system discussed in this entry all require immediate treatment, usually surgery, to prevent severe damage or death.

Fortunately, congenital digestive defects are uncommon. In general their cause is unknown. Most are considered to be accidents in the development process. Sometimes the defects occur in combination with other malformations, such as congenital heart defects. Some are associated with chromosomal abnormalities, such as Down syndrome.

Although congenital digestive system defects cannot be prevented, they may be revealed by ultrasound examination or other tests during pregnancy. Such advance notice makes it possible to prepare for surgery or other treatment after birth.

Gastrointestinal defects: The gastrointestinal (GI) tract is basically one long tube, extending from the mouth at one end to the anus at the other. During development, a blockage may occur at one or more points in the GI tract, interfering with the digestion of food and disposal of wastes. A partial blockage is called *stenosis* (steh-NOH-sihs), which means "narrowing". A state of complete closing down of the passage is called *atresia* (uh-TREE-zhuh). Atresia may in turn be either a blockage within the tube or the complete absence of part of it.

Typical locations for stenosis or atresia include:

- the esophagus, the tube that connects the mouth to the stomach; *esophageal atresia* is rare (1 in 4,500 newborns) and immediately detectable because the baby cannot swallow at all.
- the pylorus (piy-LAWR-uhs), a ring of muscle at the exit from the stomach; *pyloric stenosis* occurs in about 1 in 150 newborn boys and 1 in 750 newborn girls; two or three weeks after birth, the baby begins to vomit forcefully soon after feeding; pyloric stenosis can be confirmed with ultrasound or x-rays, after which it is corrected surgically, nearly always successfully.
- the small or large intestine; *intestinal atresia* (which occurs in about 1 in 1,500 newborns), in addition to vomiting and bloating, results in total lack of bowel movement.
- the anus, or exit from the digestive system; *imperforate anus* occurs in 1 in 5,000 births, preventing bowel movements and sometimes requiring extensive surgery to remedy.

Such obstructions do not harm the fetus before birth, when nourishment comes entirely from the mother and the GI tract has very little function. But problems soon appear when the newborn begins to feed. Stenosis may seriously impair passage of food through the GI tract, and atresia halts it altogether. Without prompt surgery for either condition, starvation, dehydration, or infection may quickly lead to death.

Abdominal wall defects: The *abdomen* (AAB-duh-muhn) is the part of the body between the bottom of the rib cage and the top of the hipbone. Abdominal (aab-DOM-uh-nuhl) wall defects are abnormal openings in the front wall of the abdomen that allow some of the intestines and other internal organs to protrude.

There are two forms of abdominal wall defects: *omphalocele* (OM-fuh-loh-seel) and *gastroschisis* (gaas-TROS-kih-sihs). An omphalocele forms at the navel, or *omphalos*. In gastroschisis, the opening is located to one side of the navel. Gastroschisis is generally the less serious of the two conditions, but there is considerable variation in both. Only a small amount of intestine may protrude, or most of the intestines plus other internal organs may be displaced. The standard treatment is surgery right after birth to prevent infection and ensure the proper function of the affected organs.

Biliary atresia: Bile is produced in the liver. It then flows through bile ducts into the small intestine for disposal. Excess bile is stored in the gallbladder, from which a second duct brings the bile to join the duct from the liver. Occasionally, around the time of birth, the ducts become blocked. The bile cannot flow to the intestine and backs up in the liver. This very rare condition, called *biliary atresia,* occurs in about 1 in 75,000 newborns.

The first sign of blockage is usually jaundice, as wastes build up in the blood. The bile pigment in the blood produces a yellowish discoloration of the skin and eyes. Progressive destruction and scarring, or cirrhosis, of the liver soon follow.

The causes of biliary atresia are not known, but the condition may result from an infection around the time of birth. It can also be caused by cystic fibrosis, which can plug the ducts with thickened mucus.

The first line of treatment is surgery to remove or replace the diseased ducts and to reconnect the liver to the intestine. If this procedure fails, the only alternative is a liver transplant.

Congenital diaphragmatic hernia: The diaphragm is a sheet of muscle that separates the abdomen and the chest. Its chief function is to serve as a kind of bellows that causes the lungs to expand and contract in breathing. But another function is to keep the abdominal organs, such as the stomach and intestines, from getting in the way of the heart and lungs. Occasionally, during early pregnancy, the diaphragm fails to form completely in the fetus, leaving a hole between the abdomen and chest through which some of the digestive organs protrude. This condition is known as a *diaphragmatic hernia.*

Such a hernia causes no problems before birth. But when the newborn tries to breathe, the displaced organs may not leave enough room for the lungs to expand properly. In the most serious instances, the hernia is so large that the lungs are not able to develop to full size.

A newborn with a severe diaphragmatic hernia is likely to need immediate assistance with breathing by means of a ventilator or mechanical heart-lung bypass (a procedure called *extracorporeal membrane oxygenation,* or ECMO). Once the baby is stabilized, the opening through the diaphragm is surgically repaired, either by sewing it shut or by covering it with a synthetic patch.

After surgery babies whose lungs were only displaced usually recover with little further intervention. Those with underdeveloped lungs remain at high risk and are likely to need continued assistance with breathing until the lungs have had time to grow to normal size.

Congenital diaphragmatic hernia used to be a leading cause of infant death. It remains a very serious condition but recent progress in treatment has greatly reduced the risk of death or lasting disability.

Hirschsprung's disease: Sometimes the nerves that control part of the large intestine fail to form, a condition called Hirschsprung's disease, or *clonic aganglionosis* (ay-GAANG-glee-uh-NOH-sihs). Without normal control the muscles of that part of the intestine cannot carry out the rhythmical, peristaltic contractions that move digested wastes along. Instead the muscles go into spasm, blocking the passage of wastes from the body and causing the intestine above the blockage to swell. Because of the pattern of nerve development for the intestines, this condition, which occurs in about 1 in 5,000 newborns, most frequently affects the rectum.

The first signs of the disease, as of other gastrointestinal obstructions, do not appear until after birth. Constipation may cause the baby to become dangerously dehydrated. The walls of the large intestine normally reabsorb most of the water from food, but when the intestine is blocked, no additional water can reach the large intestine to be reabsorbed. Furthermore, bacteria in the stationary wastes may produce a violent infection called *toxic enterocolitis*. Immediate surgery is needed to remove the paralyzed segment of the colon.

Congenital heart defects

Congenital heart defects (CHD) are among the most common of all birth defects. The defects are called *congenital* because they are present at birth.

All congenital heart defects interfere in some way with normal blood circulation and cause a shortage of oxygen (*hypoxia*) in the body. Some defects are so mild they are never noticed, while others are so severe they result in early death.

Cause: While the causes of most congenital heart defects are unknown, some are produced by prenatal exposure to antiepilepsy drugs, alcohol, or virus diseases such as rubella ("German measles"). Others are associated with chromosomal abnormalities such as Down syndrome. Most, though, occur unpredictably at an early stage of prenatal development, when the heart and blood vessels are formed.

Incidence: Congenital heart defects occur in about 1 in 200 births. About 1 million people in the United States have CHDs that have been successfully treated or that are too mild to need treatment.

Common types: At least 35 congenital heart defects are known, but most are rare. The following are among the most common.

Septal defects: The most common of all CHDs are known familiarly as "holes in the heart." They are actually holes in the central walls, or *septa*, that normally separate the chambers of the right side of the heart from those of the left. They can occur between the *atria*, which are the heart's upper chambers, or between the lower chambers, called *ventricles*, or both. The holes may be so small that they cause no symptoms or heal by themselves. But large ones seriously interfere with circulation and may cause early death if not repaired.

A normal heart. Right and left are as on a person, not as seen. Red indicates oxygen-rich blood, blue, oxygen-poor blood. Arrows indicate direction of blood flow. BELOW: Seven common defects. Purple is mixed blood.

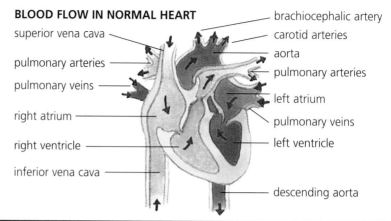

BLOOD FLOW IN NORMAL HEART

- brachiocephalic artery
- superior vena cava
- carotid arteries
- pulmonary arteries
- aorta
- pulmonary veins
- pulmonary arteries
- right atrium
- left atrium
- pulmonary veins
- right ventricle
- left ventricle
- inferior vena cava
- descending aorta

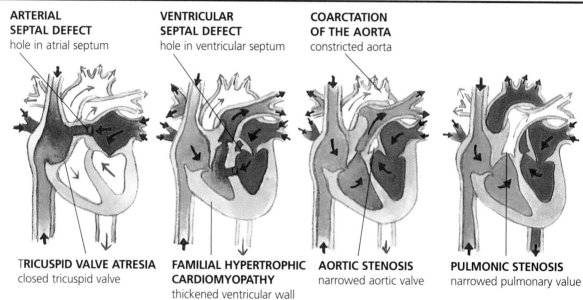

ARTERIAL SEPTAL DEFECT
hole in atrial septum

VENTRICULAR SEPTAL DEFECT
hole in ventricular septum

COARCTATION OF THE AORTA
constricted aorta

TRICUSPID VALVE ATRESIA
closed tricuspid valve

FAMILIAL HYPERTROPHIC CARDIOMYOPATHY
thickened ventricular wall

AORTIC STENOSIS
narrowed aortic valve

PULMONIC STENOSIS
narrowed pulmonary value

Pulmonary stenosis (steh-NOH-sihs, literally "narrowing"): The pulmonary artery carries blood from the heart to the lungs to pick up fresh oxygen. It has a pulmonary valve that allows blood to enter the artery but prevents it from flowing back into the heart. Pulmonary stenosis restricts the flow at or near the valve. If it is severe, not enough blood reaches the lungs, and not enough oxygen is absorbed to meet the body's needs. In such cases surgery may eventually be needed.

Aortic stenosis: The aorta is the artery that carries oxygen-enriched blood from the heart to the rest of the body. At the point where it leaves the heart is the *aortic valve*, which allows blood to flow out of the heart but not back into it. Aortic stenosis is a narrowing of the valve itself or of the aorta near it. In severe instances it may reduce the blood flow enough to cause debilitating hypoxia; it may also cause the heart to be damaged from overwork.

Coarctation of the aorta: Coarctation (KOH-ahrk-TAY-shuhn) of the aorta is a constriction of the aorta just past the point where branches lead to the upper part of the body. The blood pressure rises dangerously in these upper vessels, including those that serve the heart muscle itself, but drops in the lower ones. This is a serious defect that almost always requires surgery.

Tetralogy of Fallot (teht-RAHL-uh-jee uv fah-LOH): This is a combination of four different heart defects:

- *ventricular septal defect* (see above)
- *pulmonary stenosis* (see above)
- *overriding of the aorta,* in which the opening of the aorta is displaced to the right, over the ventricular septal defect, so that blood from both ventricles flows into it
- *hypertrophied right ventricle,* in which the right ventricle is overworked and becomes thickened, enlarged, and in danger of failure.

This combination of defects seriously interferes with circulation and usually must be repaired as soon as the child can tolerate surgery.

Tricuspid valve atresia: The tricuspid valve allows the one-way flow of blood from the right atrium to the right ventricle. Sometimes it fails to form properly during prenatal development, so that circulation to the lungs is completely blocked. The defect is quickly fatal after birth unless it is accompanied by septal defects. These allow the left side of the heart to supply blood to both the lungs and the rest of the body. The child can then live until surgery is performed.

Transposition of the great vessels: In this very serious malformation the aorta and pulmonary artery switch places. As a result, the normal cycle of blood circulation to the lungs and then to the rest of the body is broken. Oxygen-rich blood from the lungs is pumped right back to them, while "used" blood from the body is also pumped back directly, without any fresh oxygen.

Like tricuspid valve atresia, this defect is quickly fatal unless it is accompanied by other defects. These may allow a combined circulation to the lungs and body that can keep the child alive until surgery is performed.

Noticeable symptoms: Hypoxia may cause breathlessness, weakness, fatigue, chest pain (angina), and dizziness or faintness, especially during or after exertion. Serious defects may produce *cyanosis* (siy-uh-NOH-sihs), a bluish cast of the skin caused by dark, oxygen-starved blood flowing through the body. Infants suffering from cyanosis are familiarly known as "blue babies."

Diagnosis: The presence of a heart defect may be suggested by a faint pulse or a heart murmur heard through a stethoscope. Some defects can be diagnosed from an electrocardiogram (ECG). But the most definitive evidence comes from a sophisticated form of ultrasound technology known as *echocardiography.*

Treatment options: Most serious congenital heart defects can be successfully remedied by surgery. Cardiac catheterization, the insertion of a tool-tipped plastic tube through a blood vessel to the heart, can sometimes be used as a substitute or supplement to surgery. In emergencies such procedures may have to be performed during infancy, but more often they are postponed until childhood.

Congestion

SYMPTOM

The term "congestion" is used in medicine to mean a blockage, just as "traffic congestion" refers to a slow or stopped flow of automobiles. Sometimes congestion results from a swelling that blocks one of the several body tubes through which air flows, but more often it is caused by thickening of other fluids in the tubes. Sometimes there is too much fluid to flow through narrow passages, and fluid buildup follows.

Parts affected: Congestion most often affects the nasal passages or the bronchial passages that carry air into the lungs. The lungs themselves may also fill with fluid. Sinus cavities (open spaces in the skull that are connected to the nasal passages) that become congested may cause headaches.

Phone doctor

Related symptoms: Congestion of the nose or lungs interferes with breathing. Coughing frequently occurs in an effort to keep the passages to the lungs clear. Often the underlying cause of congestion is an infectious disease that results in fever or fatigue.

Sinus congestion may cause the head to feel stuffy, especially when combined with nasal congestion. When pressure within the sinuses increases, a severe headache may occur.

Associations: The primary causes of congestion are allergies or asthma, bronchitis, and infectious diseases of the respiratory system, especially the common cold and pneumonia of all types. More rarely congestion is the result of nasal administration of drugs such as cocaine or is a complication of syphilis.

Prevention and possible actions: Prevention depends on the cause of the congestion. Allergies and asthma can be treated before congestion develops, for example, but avoiding infection is the best way to prevent colds. Unless congestion of the upper throat blocks breathing completely, there is little serious threat to health; ***but lungs filling with fluid require treatment by a physician.*** Medicines called *decongestants* suppress the production of mucus, the fluid that is filling parts of the respiratory system or the sinus cavities.

Conjunctivitis

See **Pink eye**

Constipation

SYMPTOM

Phone doctor

Physicians usually define constipation as fewer than three bowel movements a week, but normal bowel habits vary greatly from person to person. Usually constipation is nothing more than a minor problem, but it can be a symptom of something more serious. ***If constipation persists for more than three days, or if you have blood in your stool, see your doctor.***

Cause: Constipation often is the result of diet or lifestyle. People who do not drink enough fluids or eat enough fruits, vegetables, and whole-grain foods tend to become constipated from time to time. Physical inactivity, perhaps as the result of an illness that leaves one bedridden, can also contribute to constipation.

Frequent use of laxatives can bring on constipation. Laxatives may clear out the bowel too completely and lead to bowel inactivity. That prompts the taking of another laxative, which again overempties the bowel and may start a cycle of frequent laxative use.

The large intestine removes water from wastes before they are expelled through the anus. The more time that wastes linger in the large intestine, the more water is removed. Therefore an attack of constipation results in dry stools that are difficult to pass.

People who have hemorrhoids may become constipated because they fear the pain that can accompany defecation during a hemorrhoid flareup. Fear of pain can also be a factor for patients with an anal fissure—a small tear in the anus. Constipation is a common problem among pregnant women. By the fourth month of pregnancy a woman's uterus has expanded enough to put pressure on the intestines and to increase the likelihood of constipation.

Children become constipated in several different situations. Infants on an all-milk diet after normal weaning time may develop hard stools because milk contains no fiber. Adding cereal or fruit to the diet usually helps.

Any disruption of normal bowel routine—while traveling, for instance—could result in constipation. Stress may also cause this problem.

Sometimes constipation is a side effect of prescription medications. Opiates, such as codeine, morphine, and heroin, prevent normal action of the bowels. A few people suffer alternating bouts of constipation and diarrhea, a condition due to irritable bowel syndrome.

Related symptoms: When constipated, you will find yourself regularly straining to make your bowels move. There is often a feeling of fullness in the abdomen and perhaps abdominal pains. A headache, nausea, and loss of appetite can accompany constipation as well. As a result of these feelings people sometimes reduce activities; this only tends to make the underlying constipation worse.

Associations: While constipation is usually a minor problem, it can be a side effect of more serious medical conditions. For example, people who have suffered a *stroke* or *paralysis* may have problems with constipation. Or someone suffering from severe depression may become constipated because he or she is eating less and not getting much physical exercise.

Constipation sometimes signals a condition called *hypothyroidism,* in which the thyroid is not producing enough of the hormone thyroxin. Other symptoms of this disorder include unexplained weight gain, sluggishness, more than usual sensitivity to cold, and dry skin or hair. ***Seek prompt medical attention for this potentially serious condition.***

Abdominal pain centered on the lower left side of the abdomen could be a sign of *diverticulitis.*

Especially for people over the age of 40, a sudden, unexplained onset of constipation might also be a warning sign of colon cancer. Your doctor will order tests if cancer is suspected.

Drink water

Prevention and possible actions: Eat high-fiber foods such as fruits, vegetables, and whole-grain bread to provide the bulk needed to ensure proper bowel action. Dried fruits, such as prunes, raisins, and figs, can be especially helpful in preventing constipation. In addition, drink plenty of fluids each day and get regular exercise.

It is desirable to establish a routine and have a bowel movement about the same time each day. In any event, never ignore the urge to defecate because you are too busy.

High fiber

Exercise

Convulsion

SYMPTOM

A convulsion is a sudden and uncontrolled episode in which many or all of the skeletal muscles contract; it is often accompanied by unconsciousness. The same symptom is also called a *seizure* or a *fit.* Often the word is used in the plural, as in "the child went into convulsions." By any name a convulsion is a striking event that may occur as a symptom of many different diseases or underlying conditions. Although it appears frightening to the observer, the symptom is not by itself necessarily dangerous.

Parts affected: The convulsion may simply affect an arm or a leg, although often it seems as if all the muscles in the body suddenly contract.

Phone doctor

Medic alert

Related symptoms: Often people injure themselves accidentally while the convulsion is in process, sometimes by biting the lips or tongue or by falling or striking some object. Otherwise there is no lasting effect from the convulsion itself, although there may be further problems from the underlying disease.

Associations: About half of all convulsions occur in childhood. Convulsion often occurs in young children as a result of either a high fever or the violent coughing of pertussis (whooping cough). Children who are engaged in a tantrum can sometimes produce convulsions, perhaps by holding their breath.

In people of all ages common causes of convulsion include epilepsy, for which convulsions are often the main symptom; diabetes, in which convulsion may result from an insulin overdose; or any other condition that interferes with the proper operation of the brain, including injury or loss of blood supply. Thus convulsion can result from such serious diseases as brain tumors or abscesses, encephalitis, meningitis, head injury, heat stroke, hardening of the brain arteries, or drug or alcohol overdose. Convulsions may also occur with chronic alcoholism, cerebral palsy, some genetic diseases, and some forms of leukemia. ***Always seek immediate medical assistance for convulsions of unknown origin.*** People who have epilepsy or diabetes often carry cards identifying their condition.

Prevention and possible actions: Most people with epilepsy or with permanent or long-term brain damage—for example, from cerebral palsy or a tumor—can take regular prescription medicines that reduce or eliminate convulsions. Make sure that the person experiencing the convulsion is somewhere safe and that there are no nearby objects that could cause harm. It is often suggested that convulsions of the whole body can best be treated by putting some object, such as a rolled-up dish towel or handkerchief, in the mouth in such a way as to prevent tongue or lip biting, but this may do more damage than good. It may be helpful to loosen a buttoned-up shirt collar or a tight belt. Do not administer alcohol or splash water in the face. Call a doctor, and wait for the convulsion to subside.

Relief of symptoms: Diabetic convulsions from insulin can be warded off with any sweet food or with fruit juice; but if a physician is present, he or she can inject glucose for immediate relief. Do not try to give food to someone who is unconscious.

COPD (chronic obstructive pulmonary disease)

DISEASE

TYPE: MECHANICAL

See also
Asthma
Bronchitis
Emphysema
Lungs
Respiratory system

COPD is a chronic, slowly progressive disease of the lungs. It commonly encompasses two conditions: chronic bronchitis and emphysema. The disease is permanent, and there is no known cure.

Parts affected: COPD results from damage to the respiratory system over a period of many years. Chronic bronchitis may cause the airways that lead from the throat to the lungs to narrow and become clogged with mucus. This prevents air from reaching the lungs. Emphysema damages and destroys the *alveoli*. These are the thin-walled cavities in the lungs where the exchange of oxygen to and carbon dioxide from the blood takes place.

Types: Either or both chronic bronchitis and emphysema may be present in COPD. COPD does not include asthma.

Causes: Smoking is the predominant cause of COPD, although not all smokers develop the disease. Long-term exposure to chemical fumes and certain dusts (grain, cotton, wood, mining) can contribute to COPD. Childhood respiratory illnesses also can be a risk factor.

Incidence: Because COPD develops slowly, it primarily afflicts people age 50 and older. It is the fourth leading cause of death in the United States, accounting for approximately 125,000 deaths annually. The death rate has increased dramatically in recent decades. It grew from 15.2 deaths per 100,000 in 1970 to 45.5 deaths per 100,000 in 1999. Smokers are ten times more likely than nonsmokers to die of COPD.

Noticeable symptoms: The main symptom of COPD is shortness of breath accompanied by coughing or wheezing. COPD is a "silent disease": Much damage to the respiratory system may already have occurred before symptoms become noticeable. Once symptoms appear, they may progress rapidly and become incapacitating. Walking, dressing, and other daily activities may cause extreme shortness of breath.

Diagnosis: A patient will be asked to inhale as deeply as possible, then exhale as rapidly and completely as possible. The physician will time the length of exhalation and listen for wheezing and other noises. Blood tests and other studies are used to indicate the stage of the disease.

Treatment options: Although COPD cannot be cured, its progression and severity can be controlled. Smokers will be advised to stop smoking immediately. Exercise programs to strengthen muscles will be prescribed. Lifestyle changes may be recommended to reduce stress on the respiratory system. For instance, patients may be advised to live on one floor and to avoid being around persons who smoke. Medication will be prescribed to control coughing, mucus production, and other symptoms. Supplemental oxygen and mechanical breathing assistance may be required in advanced cases. Lung transplants are an option if severe emphysema is the primary manifestation of COPD.

Don't smoke

Prevention and possible actions: The most important way to avoid COPD is to avoid smoking. People who continue to smoke should limit exposure to pollution, including occupational hazards such as dusts and chemical fumes.

Coronary thrombosis

See **Heart attack**

Coughs

SYMPTOM

A cough is a noisy expulsion of air that occurs as the result of irritation of the throat, trachea, or bronchial tubes. Its function is to clear these airways of the substance causing the irritation—particles of dust or smoke, incorrectly swallowed food, substances such as alcohol or pepper, or the thick mucus called phlegm that is produced by the body itself.

Most coughs are of no lasting significance, but coughs that persist for more than a few days may indicate more serious underlying factors.

Mechanism: Sometimes a cough results from a voluntary decision to expel air—for example, to attract attention—but most coughs are involuntary. Sensitive tissue lining the breathing passages signals irritation to the cough center in the brain. This triggers an automatic sequence of events:

- The brain signals the chest and abdominal muscles to tighten, and simultaneously orders the glottis, a narrow opening at the top of the larynx, to close.
- This combination of squeezing of muscles and closing of the "stopper" causes air pressure to build up in the lungs until it reaches explosive strength.
- The glottis is forced open, and the trapped air explodes outward at speeds as fast as 75 to 100 miles per hour.

Materials that travel on that air may go many feet before they come to rest unless the individual covers his or her mouth with a hand or a tissue. Such dispersion is particularly significant when the cough is transporting an infectious agent.

An involuntary cough may be either *productive* or *nonproductive*. The productive type of cough brings up, or produces, mucus or other materials. A nonproductive cough—also known as a dry cough—is one that does not expel anything but air. While the common cold may cause a productive cough, the cough that often comes with influenza is nonproductive.

When a cough results from an infection in the throat, a nonproductive cough can cause more harm than good. A more serious secondary infection such as bronchitis or pneumonia can follow if irritants are not dispatched in due time by a productive cough. The germs causing the disease can find their way to the lungs.

Associations: Various diseases that once occurred commonly in childhood have cough as one of their symptoms. The childhood viral diseases collectively known as croup are named for the characteristic barklike cough. As is the case for croup, pertussis (whooping cough) is characterized by a distinctive pattern and sound. Other diseases, including measles, may include coughing as a symptom.

Life-threatening diseases that have cough among other symptoms include pneumonias of all kinds and tuberculosis

Phone doctor

(measles may also be life-threatening). Coughs that produce blood are markers of potentially serious conditions and should be investigated by a physician.

Another relatively common type of cough is that which occurs among heavy smokers or former smokers. That cough may become so familiar a part of the individual's life as to go unnoticed. It is usually the result of chronic high levels of abnormally thick mucus in the lower bronchial airways caused by the constant presence of irritants in cigarettes and other tobacco products. The smokers' cough maybe a forerunner of other more serious conditions beginning with bronchitis and escalating to emphysema and lung and throat cancers.

Relief of symptoms: There are two basic kinds of medications that have been used to treat coughs: *suppressants,* also called antitussives, and *expectorants.*

The goal of a cough suppressant is to silence a nonproductive cough, either through narcotic or nonnarcotic agents that lull the brain's cough center to be less responsive to signals of irritation. Cough suppressants come in liquid form and in medicated hard candies, variously known as lozenges, trochees, and drops, designed to be absorbed slowly in the mouth. Anything that suppresses a cough should be used only for a day or two, according to package instructions, since coughs are a necessary function of the body.

The most effective narcotic substance for cough relief, sold in strength only by prescription, is codeine, a derivative of opium. Because codeine is potentially addictive, has many side effects, and can interact with other medical conditions in even tiny concentrations, even over-the-counter medications containing codeine should not be taken without consulting your physician. Somewhat less powerful but much safer is the synthetic cough suppressant dextromethorphan.

The goal of expectorant medications is to decrease the stickiness of thick or viscous mucus and thereby make it looser in the throat and easier to be coughed up. A panel of professionals convened by the U.S. Food and Drug Administration (FDA) to test the effectiveness of expectorants on coughs found little evidence to support the use of common medications except for those containing guaifenesin.

A cough propels germs into the atmosphere where they can travel many feet before landing on a surface or another person. Since many germs can live on surfaces for a long time and still be infectious, the person coughing can lower the risk of his disease spreading by covering his mouth with a tissue each time he coughs.

The FDA panel also asserted that cough medicines that combine suppressant and expectorant drugs are a bad idea because, at best, they counteract each other.

For the cough due to a cold or other minor nose-and-throat illnesses the best treatment may be drinking lots of fluids, using a room air humidifier, and sleeping with the head slightly elevated.

Cowpox

See **Animal diseases and humans**

Cramp

SYMPTOM

See also
Circulatory system
Cryptosporidiosis
Diabetes mellitus, type I ("juvenile")
Diabetes mellitus, type II ("adult-onset")
Diet and disease
Fatigue
Gastroenteritis
Leg cramps
Menstrual pain
Muscles
Parkinson's disease
Skeletal muscles
Smooth muscles
Spinal cord
Stomachache
Whipworm

Cramp is a spasm and involuntary contraction of a muscle. Although cramps can be quite painful, they are usually harmless.

Parts affected: Any skeletal muscle may become cramped from strenuous or repetitious exertion. Cramps in the feet, legs, abdomen, arms, and hands are all fairly common. People who do not exercise often enough or who abruptly increase the amount they exercise may experience a skeletal muscle cramp during or even some time after a workout. The possible activities that cause cramp are diverse, ranging from jogging (leg cramp) to writing by hand (writer's cramp). Abdominal cramps are generally caused by contractions in the smooth muscles, such as the uterus (menstrual pain) or the stomach and intestines (indigestion or gastroenteritis).

Related symptoms: Cramp caused by physical activity usually is accompanied by a sharp or aching pain and a slight bulging of the affected muscle. Abdominal cramps caused by gastroenteritis may be accompanied by nausea, diarrhea, and fever.

Heat cramp is a skeletal muscle contraction caused by sweating. With heat cramp the patient may also have a weak pulse and dilated pupils.

Causes and associations: Heat cramp is brought on by loss of salt through sweating.

Nighttime cramping in legs and feet while lying in bed, called *recumbency cramp,* may follow strenuous exercise earlier in the day or perhaps be a result of aging (as people age, their muscles tend to cramp more easily). Recumbency cramp may also occur in people with Parkinson's disease, diabetes, and spinal cord lesions and in those receiving dialysis and some types of chemotherapy.

Leg cramp or pain that occurs while walking short distances, and that quickly goes away when walking stops, is known as *claudication,* a symptom of clogged arteries in the legs also known as *peripheral vascular disease. Hypocalcemia,* a disease associated with calcium deficiency, also causes extensive muscle cramping.

Abdominal cramping may precede labor or accompany menstrual periods. Stomach or colon cancers also produce abdominal cramping, as do the parasites whipworms. But the most common cause is a viral infection of the digestive system, called gastroenteritis (sometimes known as stomach flu).

Prevention and possible actions: Drink water or other liquids before and during exercise to help prevent cramping. Stretch muscles before exercising vigorously. Gradually increase your workout instead of trying to do too much at once. In hot weather wear lightweight, loose-fitting clothing, and rest more frequently.

Relief of symptoms: Cramp usually lasts only a few minutes and often goes away by itself. Massaging the affected muscle may relieve the pain and help relax the muscle more quickly. Recumbency cramp can often be relieved by standing and walking a few steps. For heat cramp move to a shaded area, and drink water mixed with salt.

Cretinism

See **Hormone disorders**

Creutzfeldt-Jakob disease

(KROITS-fehlt YAH-kop)

DISEASE

TYPE: INFECTIOUS (PRION)

Although Creutzfeldt-Jakob disease (CJD) has historically been rare, recent developments have combined to make it better known than many more common fatal diseases. Some famous people have died from the disease, notably the choreographer George Balanchine, who succumbed in 1983. An outbreak in the 1980s occurred when some people received human growth hormone that had been infected with the disease. The epidemic of mad cow disease in Great Britain in the 1990s led to infection with a variant of CJD.

Cause: Some cases of CJD appear to be sporadic—that is, they arise independent of any known cause in an individual. One form is thought to be genetic. Other instances arise from infection from a known source.

Transmission of CJD is similar to that of a virus, but the disease takes from 10 to 50 years to develop. Contamination of the human growth hormone probably occurred at least 8 and perhaps as many as 20 years before disease symptoms were observed in the mid-1980s. Therefore the causative agent of CJD was originally labeled a "slow" virus. But in 1985 neurologist Stanley B. Prusiner proposed that "slow viruses" are a form of protein and not viruses at all. He christened the aberrant protein form a prion (PREE-on). The prion is an altered form of a normal protein found in the brain. It has the unusual ability of transmitting its altered form to the normal protein, resulting in all of the normal protein of that type gradually changing into prions.

Incidence: CJD is rare, with one person in every million diagnosed worldwide each year, about 6,000 cases annually. In the United States the number developing the disease is about 200 each year. The symptoms appear mostly in people between 55 and 80. Men and women are affected about equally.

Noticeable symptoms: CJD begins with the mental confusion and forgetting called dementia, somewhat as in the more familiar syndrome Alzheimer's disease. Progression once symptoms appear is much faster, however, and the dementia is combined with effects on the muscles, including loss of muscle mass (known as "wasting") and movement of various parts of the body without conscious control. There may be an unusually stiff gait, difficulty in speech, hallucinations, and loss of memory as well.

Diagnosis: In addition to specific tests for dementia or muscle changes, computerized tomography (CT) brain scans can be used to determine that the brain tissue is becoming defective. Other tests, such as a spinal taps, are used to rule out possible other causes of symptoms. In later stages an electroencephalogram reveals patterns in brain waves that are specific to the disease and that confirm diagnosis. A biopsy can sometimes reveal characteristic signs in the brain, which can be confirmed after death by a brain autopsy.

Treatment options: There is no known treatment, although medications can help control such symptoms as aggressiveness or loss of muscle control.

Stages and progress: In the classic form of CJD symptoms begin to appear in middle age; young people do not get this disease in part because the infection grows so slowly. After symptoms begin, the progression is rapid, with notable degeneration from week to week. Death usually occurs within six months, although sometimes the victim may live for one or two years.

Prevention: Extra sterilization or destruction of instruments used to treat or diagnose persons with known CJD is needed to prevent transmission. Growth hormone is manufactured by genetic engineering, so it cannot become contaminated. Careful screening is used to eliminate other possible sources of transmission, such as transplants.

Crohn's disease

DISEASE

TYPE: AUTOIMMUNE;
      GENETIC

A chronic inflammation of the intestines, Crohn's disease causes intermittent bouts of diarrhea, abdominal cramps, and low-grade fever. Attacks can be largely controlled with medical treatment, but the disease itself cannot be cured. Eventually, serious complications can develop; over half of those with the disease will need to have corrective surgery.

Cause: Medical experts do not know exactly what causes Crohn's disease, but there is a greater chance of developing the disease when a family history exists. About 20% of people with the disease have a close relative that also has it. Many share a mutation of the gene *Nod2* on chromosome 16 that increases the chance of developing the disease from two to thirty times.

Recurring inflammation in a part or parts of the intestine is characteristic of the disease. The inflammation is probably induced by an abnormal response by the immune system. The protein produced by *Nod2*, for example, attacks harmful bacteria, but appears to attack benign microorganisms as well when the gene has a Crohn's mutation. The immune system may also attack the lining of the intestine.

Incidence: Once rare, Crohn's disease is becoming more common—the number of cases reported has doubled in the past 30 years, with 30,000 Americans diagnosed with the disease annually. In Western nations from 1 to 3 persons in 1,000 develop the disease. Symptoms appear during teenage or young-adult years in most cases—90% of all patients develop the disease by age 40.

Noticeable symptoms: Periodic bouts of cramping in the lower right section of the abdomen (mimicking appendicitis), diarrhea, bloody or black tarlike stools, nausea, a low-grade fever, and a general feeling of ill health or weakness are characteristic symptoms of Crohn's disease. The patient may also experience some abdominal swelling and tenderness. Mouth lesions are common, and about a third of patients also develop anal abscesses.

Diagnosis: When Crohn's disease is suspected, it is important that a medical history of the patient's family be taken to determine whether there may be other members with similar symptoms. If so, there is a greater chance that symptoms signal Crohn's disease rather than ulcerative colitis or another condition producing similar symptoms, irritable bowel syndrome.

Other symptoms that appear only in more advanced cases of Crohn's disease may help doctors make a diagnosis. For example, x-rays may show development of abscesses and small tubelike passages leading from the small intestine to the colon, stomach, or other locations. The inside of the small intestine may also become narrower because scar tissue has formed after repeated bouts of inflammation.

Treatment options: No cure for Crohn's disease exists, but medical treatment can ease the effects of the recurring attacks. Medications reduce symptoms of Crohn's disease. Antidiarrheal and antispasmodic drugs usually reduce the patient's diarrhea and abdominal cramps. Corticosteroids have proven effective for reducing inflammation in active flareups; they may also be used in smaller doses over the long term to prevent new attacks. But long-term use of steroids may produce serious side effects, including in the more extreme instances diabetes, cataracts, osteoporosis, and hypertension. Immune-system-suppressing drugs may also be effective against Crohn's disease.

No stress

Emotional stress appears to play a part in Crohn's disease, and treatment often includes changing the patient's daily routine to reduce stress wherever possible. Nutrition is also important. Vitamin supplements and a well-balanced diet are recommended. Unless the patient's small intestine has narrowed due to scarring, the doctor may prescribe fiber supplements as well.

Eventually, a surgeon may have to remove the affected part of the small or large intestine because repeated attacks scar the bowel and cause other medical complications.

Surgery can produce dramatic improvement, but the results are often temporary. Flareups occur in another part of the intestine in over half the patients who have surgery. Repeated surgical removal of inflamed parts of the intestine can shorten the small intestine so drastically that it is no longer able to absorb enough nourishment; after that the patient must be fed intravenously.

Stages and progress: The first attacks of Crohn's disease often appear when the patient is in his or her twenties. About a quarter of those who get the disease have only one or two attacks and never experience any further problems. But for the rest, attacks may recur at varying intervals ranging from months to several years.

In about a third of all cases there is chronic inflammation of the small intestine only, usually just the final section. Half the cases show inflammation in both the small and large intestines, usually in the end of the small intestine and upper part of the large.

About one out of every five persons with Crohn's disease develops *enteric arthritis,* pain that tends to move from one joint to another, often affecting the spine. Unlike other forms of arthritis, symptoms often vanish after a few months.

INDEX

A

Abdominal wall defects **2:**99
Abruptio placentae **7:**5, **7:**10, **7:**14
Abscess **1:9–10**, **2:**16–17, **7:**35
Acetaminophen **6:**58
Achalasia **2:**56, **3:**102
Achilles tendon **8:**67–68
Achlorhydria **8:**22
Achondroplasia **4:**104, **7:**84–85
Acid reflux **4:**40
Acne **1:10–12**
Acoustic neuroma **3:**52, **8:**85
Acromegaly **4:**104, **6:**99
ACTH (adrenocorticotropic hormone) **4:**102
Actinomycetes **1:**97
Acupuncture **6:**59
Acute inflammatory polyneuropathy. *See* Guillain-Barré syndrome
Acute lymphocytic leukemia **5:**56
Acute nonlymphocytic leukemia **5:**56
Acute porphyrias **7:**3–4
Acute pyelonephritis **5:**36
Acyclovir **2:**88, **4:**36
ADA deficiency **1:12–13**, **5:**3
Addiction **3:**57, **3:**59–60
Addison, Thomas **4:**106
Addison's disease **1:**17, **1:**91, **4:**104, **4:**106, **8:**22
Adenine **4:**38
Adenoids **6:**26, **8:**62
Adenoma **8:**85
Adenomyosis **3:**90
Adenosine deaminase. *See* ADA deficiency
Adenoviruses **1:**87, **8:**103
ADH (antidiuretic hormone) **3:**29, **4:**103, **6:**98
Adrenal glands **1:16–17**, **3:**89, **6:**77–78
ADHD (attention-deficit/hyperactivity disorder) **1:13–15**
Adrenaline. *See* Epinephrine
Adult acne. *See* Rosacea
Aedes aegypti (mosquito) **3:**20
African sleeping sickness **6:**72
Afterbirth. *See* Placenta
Agent Orange **2:**66
Agoraphobia **6:**63

Agranulocytes **6:**92
Agranulocytosis **6:**24
AIDS (acquired immunodeficiency syndrome) **1:17–22**, **8:**13, **8:**15–16
and blood transfusions **1:**46
entry through birth canal **1:**109
history **1:**21
HIV testing **1:**19
and immune system **5:**4, **5:**5
as modern pandemic **3:**98
opportunistic diseases **6:**39–40
Pneumocystis carinii **1:**20, **6:**105–6
AIDS dementia **1:**20
Air sac **5:**66
Albinism **1:22–24**, **7:**104
Alcohol
and cancer **2:**35
fetal alcohol syndrome **1:**28, **3:116–17**
and frostbite **4:**19–20
nausea from **6:**14
Alcoholics Anonymous **1:**25, **1:**27, **5:**100
Alcoholism **1:24–29**
alcoholic siderosis **7:**88
and cirrhosis of the liver **2:**75
delirium tremens **1:**25, **3:16–17**
dementia **3:**19–20
Korsakoff's syndrome **1:**42
pancreatitis **6:**62–63
paranoia **6:**68
Alcohol poisoning **1:**24
ALD (adrenoleukodystrophy) **1:29–30**
Aldosterone **1:**16, **4:**102
Allele **4:**39
Allergens **1:**30–34, **1:**74, **4:**60
Allergic contact dermatitis **7:**32
Allergic purpura **7:**26
Allergic rhinitis. *See* Hay fever
Allergies **1:30–34**
from animals **6:**89
asthma **1:73–77**
hay fever **1:**31, **4:60–62**
and immune system **5:**3

and itching **5:**26
to stings **8:**20, **8:**21
Allodynia **7:**80
Alper, Tikva **7:**16
Alpha interferon **4:**90
ALS (amyotrophic lateral sclerosis) **1:34–37**, **6:**65
Altitude sickness. *See* Polycythemia
Alveoli **2:**109, **3:**82–83, **5:**66, **7:**39
Alzheimer's disease **1:37–40**
dementia **3:**19–20
Amblyopia **3:**106–7
Amebic dysentery **1:**9, **3:**60–62, **6:**72
Amenorrhea **1:40–41**
Amino acids **4:**39
Amnesia **1:41–43**, **2:**96
Amniocentesis **2:**70
Amniotic fluid **3:**117, **7:**12–13
Amphetamines **3:**58
Amyloidosis **8:**31–32
Amyotrophic lateral sclerosis. *See* ALS
Analgesia **7:**78
Anal itching **5:**26
Anaphylactic shock **1:**32, **7:**83, **8:**31
Anaphylaxis **5:**44
Anemia(s) **1:43–47**, **3:**114
aplastic **1:**44
pernicious **1:**44, **8:**22
in pregnancy **7:**9
thalassemia **1:**44, **8:46–47**
See also Sickle cell anemia
Anencephaly **6:**22
Anesthetics, local **6:**59
Aneurysm **1:47–49**, **2:**75, **5:**25, **8:**27
Angina **1:50–51**, **2:**40
Angiography **1:**79, **3:**75–76
Angioplasty **1:**80, **4:**79
Angiotensin **3:**33
Angle-closure glaucoma **4:**47
Animal bites **1:**54, **6:**91
snakebites **7:112–14**
spider bites **8:1–2**
Animal diseases and humans **1:51–55**
anthrax **1:**54, **1:58–61**
cryptosporidiosis **3:4–5**
Q fever **7:27–28**
rabies **1:**51, **1:**53, **6:**89, **7:29–30**

tularemia **8:84**
See also Pets and disease
Animal models **1:**54
Ankylosing spondylitis **1:**93, **1:**95
Anopheles mosquito **5:**80
Anorexia nervosa **1:55–58**
Anosmia **6:**26–27, **7:**78
Ant **8:**20
Antegrade amnesia **1:**41
Anterior compartment syndrome **4:**17
Anthracosis **3:**94
Anthrax **1:**54, **1:58–61**
bioterrorism **3:**81
Antibiotics
for gonorrhea **4:**49
for infants **5:**9
Antibodies **5:**2–3, **5:**75, **6:**92–93
in rheumatoid arthritis **7:**46
Anticoagulants **3:**76
Anticonvulsants **3:**100, **6:**58
Antidepressants **6:**58
Antidiuretic hormone. *See* ADH
Antigens **1:**32
Antihistamines **4:**61–62, **4:**99
Anti-inflammatory drugs **6:**58
Antipsychotic drugs **7:**68–69
Antiretrovirals **1:**19
Antivenin **7:**113
Anus **2:**98, **3:**47, **7:**35
Anuscope **4:**87
Anxiety **1:61–63**, **5:**99
Aorta **1:**70, **6:**79
coarctation of **2:**103
overriding of **2:**103
transposition of great vessels **2:**103–4
Aortic aneurysm **1:**47–49
Aortic stenosis **2:**102–3, **4:**69
Aortic valve **2:**102–3
Aphasia **1:63–64**
Aphthous ulcer **2:**38
Aplastic anemia **1:**44–45
Aplastic crisis **7:**87
Apnea **2:**62
See also Sleep apnea
Apocrine glands **3:**105
Apoplexy. *See* Stroke
Appendicitis **1:64–66**, **3:**48, **8:**23
Appendicular skeleton **7:**96–97

Our thanks to the following organizations and persons who made the photographs used in this set possible:

Christ Episcopal Church Youth Program (Mary Millan)
Mount Vernon Teen Task Force (Chris Webb)
Putnam Family Support and Advocacy, Inc. (Pam Forde)

Photography assistant: Tania Gandy-Collins

MODELS
Roland Benson, Sally Bunch, Deirdre Burke, Kevin Chapin, Michael Clarke, Michelle Collins, Bryan Duggan, Germaine Elvy, Caitlin Faughnan, Imgard Kallenbach, Max Lipson, Lydia McCarthy, Amanda Moradel, Joshua Moradel, Veronica Moradel, Kate Peckham, Sara Pettinger, Mario Salinas, Heather Scogna, Halima Simmons, Wendy Sinclair, T.J. Trancynger, Rolando Walker, Deborah Whelan, Gregory Whelan, Francis Wick, Elaine Young, Leanne Young